MW01247420

# -DO-
# YOU?

**BUSINESS THE YAHOO! WAY**

## ANTHONY VLAMIS & BOB SMITH

# -DO-
# YOU?

## BUSINESS THE YAHOO! WAY
### SECRETS OF THE WORLD'S MOST POPULAR INTERNET COMPANY

CAPSTONE

Copyright © Anthony Vlamis and Robert Smith 2001

The right of Anthony Vlamis and Robert Smith to be identified as the authors of
this work has been asserted in accordance with the Copyright, Designs and Patents
Act 1988

First published 2001 by
Capstone Publishing, Inc.          Capstone Publishing Limited
40 Commerce Park                   8 Newtec Place
Milford                            Oxford OX4 1RE
CT 06460                           United Kingdom
USA                                http://www.capstone.co.uk
Contact: info@capstonepub.com

All rights reserved. Except for the quotation of short passages for the purposes of
criticism and review, no part of this publication may be reproduced, stored in a
retrieval system, or transmitted, in any form or by any means, electronic, mechanical,
photocopying, recording or otherwise, without the prior permission of the publisher.

CIP catalogue records for this book are available from the British Library
and the US Library of Congress.
Library of Congress Card Number: 00-109578

ISBN 1-84112-111-8

Typeset in 11/15 pt New Baskerville by
Sparks Computer Solutions Ltd, Oxford, UK
http://www.sparks.co.uk
Printed and bound by
Sheridan Books, Ann Arbour, Michigan

This book is printed on acid-free paper

Substantial discounts on bulk quantities of Capstone books are available to
corporations, professional associations and other organizations. If you are in the
USA or Canada, phone the LPC Group, Special Sales Department for details on
(1-800-626-4330) or fax (1-800-334-3892). Everywhere else, phone Capstone
Publishing on (+44-1865-798623) or fax (+44-1865-240941).

# CONTENTS

# DEDICATION AND ACKNOWLEDGMENTS

This book is dedicated to your business success. I hope that the information and insights we've gleaned from the triumphs of Yahoo! will inspire and guide you to achieve all that you desire.

My own success in turning this book from idea to reality comes from the wealth of love and support I receive from my family. I especially want to thank my parents, Connie and Earl Smith, who have always been there for me during both the good and bad times, as well as my sister, Elaine Smith, for being such a good friend and sounding board in my life. A special note of thanks goes to my partner, Tom Moffit, without a doubt my best friend and greatest supporter for more than 14 years. And last but certainly not least, to our agent John Willig, and to co-author Tony Vlamis for his professional alliance and personal friendship throughout this project and many more to come.

– Bob Smith

Many thanks to those without whose words of encouragement, inspiration and understanding this book would not have been possible. To my two greatest assets in life, Connie my wife and friend, and son Steven Alexander who thought it was cool to write about Yahoo! To my parents, Steve and Anne, and sister Suzanne,whose enthusiasm sustained me. To our agent, John Willig, for bringing us the project. Special thanks to Alex Saenz for research and help with Chapter 4 and to Bob Smith, a co-author who is a true collaborator, writing partner, and inspirational online comrade.

– Anthony Vlamis

---◆---

Introduction

# YAHOO! WE'RE RICH!

---◆---

Some say it was success by accident. Others see it as the classic story of a Silicon Valley startup. And there are those who even tout it as the digital Horatio Alger tale of our time.

The story of Yahoo! is one that must be told because it combines an interesting array of elements and people coming together to make it happen. What started as a hobby between two graduate engineering students at Stanford University today ranks as one of the world's leading Internet media companies that offers a branded network of media, commerce and communication services to more than 156 million users worldwide ( Yahoo! FQ2 2000 report) via a growing global network that includes 23 world properties.

Yahoo! continues to wow investors with strong growth, in terms of both revenue and traffic. Revenue jumped a whopping 110 percent between 1999 and 2000, from $128 million to $270 million. At the same time, the number of page views spiraled at a rate of 40 percent, from 465 million per day in December 1999 to 625 million in March 2000.

Even more appealing for analysts is Yahoo!'s gross margins of 86 percent. With $1.2 billion in cash, the company owns a mere $64 million in property, plant and equipment. (Motley Fool, April 6, 2000)

These are pretty impressive statistics for a company that, according to its founders, was born solely as a fun way to avoid doing their doctoral dissertations. And it certainly has made them extremely wealthy in the process. According to *Fortune* magazine's inaugural list of *America's 40 Richest Under Forty*, 33-year-old David Filo holds the number 5 spot, having amassed some $3.12 billion in wealth. His partner, 30-year-old Jerry Yang, follows closely behind in the number 6 position with $3.05 billion.

Could such tremendous wealth and success actually happen by accident? Is this the classic American rags-to-riches story? Does Yahoo! represent a prime example of the Silicon Valley basement-to-big-business model?

We believe Yahoo! incorporates aspects from all three scenarios. True, the company can trace its roots to "basement" beginnings, although in this case it's actually a trailer. The individuals involved did not come from wealthy backgrounds. And, yes, you could say there was a little luck thrown in.

But more important, the guiding principles that continue to drive Yahoo! – established by its founders and supported by other key players within the company – make this a valuable study in business management for the Internet economy. If it weren't for the vision, expertise and strategic style of the people behind Yahoo! – particularly its two chief Yahoos! – this certainly would have been a very different story.

## HUMBLE BEGINNINGS

Jerry Yang was ten years old when he emigrated from Taiwan to the US with his mother Lily and younger brother Ken (his father having died eight years earlier). The family arrived in San José, California. While his mom worked as a maid to support the family, Yang easily settled into the local school system as a straight-A student.

Meanwhile, David Filo was growing up with his architect father, Jerry, and his accountant mother, Carol, in Moss Bluff, Louisiana. During his childhood years, the Filo family lived in an alternative community, sharing a garden and a kitchen with six other families.

Their two paths did not cross until many years later at Stanford University. Filo, who had completed undergraduate studies in computer engineering at Tulane University in New Orleans, arrived on campus following his decision to earn a master's degree in electrical engineering. Yang, who had completed his undergraduate studies at Stanford in electrical engineering, stayed on for his master's degree. Both received their MS degrees in 1990 and soon started sharing an office in a campus trailer as electrical engineering PhD candidates. Yang and Filo worked in the same electronic computer-aided design research group and supported themselves as Stanford resident assistants.

**Yahoo!'s founders are the first to admit that creating a business was the furthest thing from their minds when they started ...**

## A labor of love

As students, the Internet became a daily part of their lives, starting with email and newsgroup postings, followed by Gopher – a pre-Web system developed at the University of Minnesota – that organized and displayed content available on Internet servers as a hierarchically structured list of files. But it wasn't until 1993 when the two got their hands on the earliest version of Mosaic – the first Web browser application developed by the National Center for Supercomputing Applications – that the future of Yahoo! appeared on the horizon.

By the end of the year, Filo's personal list of "bookmarked" Web sites had outnumbered 200. And Mosaic's "hot list" feature could not organize all these Web-site links into convenient on-screen folders. So Yang and Filo decided to write some software that would help them locate, identify and edit Web-based content so their growing list could be organized into subject areas.

**"It just grew by word of mouth and by people linking to it from their home pages." – David Filo**

Yahoo!'s founders are the first to admit that creating a business was the furthest thing from their minds when they started to compile the list. "David and I were just fooling around on the Internet, making our own database of Web sites and clicking them onto our page," Yang recalled during a 1997 interview with *Money* magazine. "We didn't know what our list was worth. We just liked doing it." (*Money*, October 1, 1997)

Filo agrees, noting that Yahoo!'s beginning was solely a means for the two of them to keep track of Web sites that they found interesting. And at the start, it wasn't something they were willing to share. "It was just between us at first," Filo said during a May 1995 interview with Sun Microsystems' *What's Happening* newsletter (*What's Happening*, June 1995). But the duo did eventually float their directory on the Internet, using their two student workstations, which they named after two famous Hawaiian sumo wrestlers. Yang's computer, named *akebono*, ran the original directory, while Filo's computer, named *konishiki*, ran the search engine. Even then, they never bothered to list their directory on any other Web sites or newsgroups. "A couple of friends started to use it," Filo added. "It just grew by word of mouth and by people linking to it from their home pages."

Although their directory (originally titled *Jerry and David's Guide to the World Wide Web* before they renamed it *Yahoo!*) was born as a hobby, not as a business, its potential did not escape the two graduate students. "I think from day one, we believed the potential of what we created [was] huge," Yang told CNNfn correspondent Valerie Morris in 1997 (September 24, 1997). "So David and I really took this as a hobby, a labor of love if you will, for about a year and a half before we decided that we should take some venture capital and try to do this as a business ourselves."

## Getting into shape

Early 1995 proved a pivotal time for Yahoo! For starters, Marc Andreessen, co-founder of Netscape Communications, offered Yang and Filo the opportunity to move their files over to larger computers housed at the company's Mountain View, California-based offices. This move, according to the company's history, proved beneficial to both Yahoo!'s founders and the university from which they took a leave of absence (neither Yang nor Filo received their doctorates). Stanford's computer network, which was suffering under the weight of increasing traffic to the directory, returned to normal. Even better, Andreessen was so impressed by Yahoo! that he made it the default directory

for Netscape's Navigator Web browser. Net-heads came to the
site in droves, and Yahoo!'s legendary status began to take
shape. But others in the business world were eyeing the site
as well.

Offers abounded. Both Netscape and America Online reportedly offered to absorb Yahoo!, but Yang and Filo turned them
down. "We didn't want to work for a big company," the pair
said during their Sun interview in 1995. "We also thought our
services would be better if Yahoo! remained an independent
entity." So, the pair opted to set their sites on attracting venture
capital. Not a bad move, considering that early 1995 proved
to be a very productive time for young entrepreneurs with an
Internet idea. They had no trouble attracting callers.

Kleiner Perkins, the largest Silicon Valley venture firm,
approached the duo but reportedly wanted them to merge with
Architext (now known as Excite), which was another search
engine created by Stanford graduates. Yang and Filo declined.
But when Mike Moritz, general partner at California-based
Sequoia Capital – which had helped fund Apple Computer and
Cisco Systems – offered to put up $1 million for a stake in the
company, the business of Yahoo! Inc. was put into gear.

Yang and Filo have said that their decision to go with Sequoia
Capital was two-fold: one certainly was the venture firm's
reputation and track record, but the other factor was its support
of the pair's vision to keep Yahoo! as a free service, not turn it
into a subscription service. "Mike supports our vision, which
is to make Yahoo! commercially viable without diminishing
the spirit that makes it so popular," Yang told Newsbytes News
Network (April 20, 1995).

In the same article, Moritz (who still serves on the company's board of directors) applauded the spirit and vision of Yahoo!'s founders which, he noted, was based on respect for the Internet community and its diverse needs. But the venture capitalist knew there was more to this arrangement. "Our attraction to Yahoo! was not only the vision of the founders, but its impressive success which happened seemingly overnight. We support David and Jerry's commitment to keep Yahoo! free for users," Mortiz said, adding his belief that gradual integration of advertising and sponsorship needed to make the venture profitable would not jeopardize that promise.

> "Mike supports our vision, which is to make Yahoo! commercially viable without diminishing the spirit that makes it so popular."
> – Jerry Yang

## Filling the talent pool

With funding secured, Yang and Filo knew the next step was to bring onboard the talent to make Yahoo! successful. Although they knew that people were needed on the business-management side – although both had anointed themselves as chief Yahoo! – the pair focused first on maintaining the science that drove their directory. One of their first additions was Srinija Srinivasan, a Stanford alumna with expertise in artificial intelligence, who – with the title Ontological Yahoo! – was put in charge of organizing the branching hierarchies that steer people to content. Today she serves as vice-president, editor-in-chief.

On the business side, Yang and Filo knew they had to gain management expertise and, along with Moritz, interviewed numerous professional managers for the job of CEO. The search was extensive and, at times, interesting since some candidates were eager to talk about how they would shake things up if given the opportunity. One reportedly told the trio that his first action would be to change the name. Naturally, they immediately scratched him from the list.

The CEO search spotlight finally focused on Tim "T.K." Koogle, a Stanford-bred engineer who at the time was president of Intermec Corporation, a Seattle-based manufacturer of data collection and data communications products. Prior to that, Koogle had spent nine years at Motorola where he held numerous executive management positions in operations and corporate venture capital. In 1999, Koogle was named chairman and continues to hold both titles.

The final addition to the initial management team in mid-1995 was chief operating officer Jeffrey "Sparky" Mallet, at the time vice-president and general manager of Novell's worldwide consumer division. Previous roles included being vice-president and founding executive team member of Reference, acquired by Word Perfect Corp. in 1992. In 1999, Mallet was named president of the company.

## In the public domain

With the management team firmly in place, an employee base exceeding 100, and no profit yet to be reported, 1996 seemed like the perfect time to go public. And Yahoo! did just that on April 11, when it offered 2.6 million shares of common stock at $13 per share. That first day of trading proved historic as the stock rose 154 percent, beating the previous first-day record of 105 percent set by Netscape. The company's market capitalization stood at $848 million. Yahoo! employees were ecstatic; management was a bit anxious over the $35 million in capital that had suddenly flowed into the company. As Yang told *Fortune*, he felt "panic – no, not panic, but anxiety" at the realization that Yahoo! now had shareholders.

The following day, however, many shareholders turned skeptical and began to bail out. The stock fell to less than half of the previous day's close, prompting Manish Shah, publisher of *IPO Maven*, to sarcastically proclaim Yahoo! as Yet Another Highly Overhyped Offering – a reference to Yahoo!'s legendary acronym, Yet Another Hierarchical Officious Oracle.

The stock price remained flat through the rest of 1996, but with the dawn of 1997 came several developments that started to propel the company toward its current leading position. For starters, Yahoo! began to see the results of its "guerilla marketing" campaign. In January of that year, Yahoo! reported that it had signed on 550 advertisers. Better yet, the company posted its first quarterly profit of $92,000. And a mere three months later, Yahoo! proudly announced that Internet surfers were using the site to view 1 billion Web pages per month.

## The rest of the story

Much has happened at Yahoo! in the ensuing three years. We'll take a look at those events in the upcoming chapters since they serve as prime examples of the following principles that have guided – and continue to guide – Yahoo!

◆ *Understand the medium and its message.* As pioneers of the first Internet search engine, Yang and Filo never lost touch with their audience or the medium they used to build their company. They remain steadfast in their vision to keep Yahoo! free for users, and to support the independent nature that online services can provide to them.

◆ *Put people first, technology second.* Yahoo! had the best name and the worst technology when it came to search engines. But Yang and Filo never wavered from their belief that the "human touch" incorporated in the Yahoo! categorization process would prove victorious. And it did.

◆ *Build local communities in the global village.* The Internet is indeed a global platform, but Yahoo! gained considerable strength through creation of local US sites that were later expanded throughout the world. The founders believed this was critical in making their service not just an online resource, but a "destination."

◆ *Give users plenty of reasons for repeat visits.* Customization has been essential in Yahoo!'s success, starting with its My Yahoo! service. Add to that a growing array of services for younger generations of Internet surfers, as well as for business and commerce. It's a big reason why traffic growth outstrips the competitors, and also a key to the fact that Yahoo! continues to record the longest average user time among all of the top-traffic Web sites.

◆ *Partner with the best.* Yahoo! takes it vision of remaining independent to heart. That's why it has amassed an extensive and constantly growing list of companies it partners with to provide services and content that users want, all designed to support its ongoing mission to provide users with the "best Web experience possible."

◆ *Buy what you need*. Sometimes it's better to acquire the technology or services you need. The key is to avoid having such acquisitions become a drain on the company's bottom line. Within the past three years, Yahoo! has acquired some 14 companies, and each purchase has given rise to positive results for the company and its shareholders.

◆ *Brand it*. According to Filo, the most important factor in Yahoo!'s success has been its name. People would remember the name, even if they had no idea what the company did. These days, Yahoo! has been able to carve out a strong brand identity worldwide as a media channel.

◆ *Promote the hell out of it*. From their catchy slogan – Do You Yahoo? – to more eclectic stunts, such as a parachutist making an online purchase or employees tattooing the company logo on various body parts, the company has never veered from its marketing strategy of "Yahoo! Everywhere." And it has successfully towed the line whilst avoiding the pitfall of overcommercialization.

◆ *Create a dynamic corporate culture*. Although every company needs some sort of structure to succeed, Yahoo! has built a fairly flat organization without much hierarchy. The work is dynamic; everybody's plates are constantly full. And decisions are made on a distributed basis.

◆ *Stay paranoid*. Yang has said that Yahoo! is in the business of tracking changes. But the company also knows that the Internet will continue to change as it evolves into a true mass-market medium. Competitors lurk everywhere, which requires being flexible and ableto rethink services and new outlets to meet the changing needs and demands of customers.

## YAHOO! TIMELINE OF KEY EVENTS

◆ 1990: Jerry Yang and David Filo receive their MS degrees in electrical engineering from Stanford University and later become part of the same research group as PhD candidates.

◆ 1993: Yang and Filo begin compiling a directory of favorite Web sites, write software to help them search and categorize their "guide," and post it on their own Web page.

◆ April 1994: Yahoo! is officially born as Yang and Filo rename their directory.

◆ January 1995: Marc Andreessen, co-founder of Netscape, offers to host Yahoo! and make it the default directory for the company's Navigator Web browser.

◆ April 1995: Yahoo! receives $1 million investment from venture capital firm Sequoia Capital.

◆ August 1995: After hiring Tim Koogle as CEO and Jeff Mallet as COO, the management team writes its first business plan.

◆ April 11, 1996: Yahoo! issues IPO of 2.6 million shares at $13 per share. By close of trading, the stock has jumped 154 percent.

◆ April 12, 1996: Investors start to bail out, and Yahoo! stock drops to half of the previous trading day's price.

◆ January 14, 1997: Yahoo! posts its first quarterly profit of $92,000.

◆ April 1997: PC Meter survey cites Yahoo! as the number 1 search and directory guide for the Internet.

◆ May 7, 1997: Yahoo! announces that traffic across all Yahoo! properties reached 1 billion page views during the preceding month.

◆ July 29, 1997: Yahoo! announces 3-for-2 stock split.

◆ November 10, 1997: Mediamark Research Inc. cites Yahoo! as the online service with the largest US audience: 25.4 million unique visitors representing 63 percent of all adults using the Web.

◆ January 14, 1998: Yahoo! announces fourth quarter pro forma net income of $0.05 per share.

◆ April 8, 1998: Yahoo! traffic reaches new record of 95 million page views per day during the month of March, a 46 percent increase.

◆ July 8, 1998: Yahoo! announces 2-for-1 stock split.

◆ December 17, 1998: More than 3000 merchants participate in Yahoo! Shopping one month after its launch.

◆ January 12, 1999: Yahoo! announces 2-for-1 stock split; Tim Koogle is named chairman and Jeff Mallet is named president.

◆ May 25, 1999: More than 5000 merchants have taken advantage of Yahoo! Store commerce solution.

◆ December 27, 1999: Orders to Yahoo! Shopping increase more than 385 percent on the previous year.

◆ January 11, 2000: Yahoo! reports audience doubled in 1999 and now exceeds 120 million unique users.

◆ January 11, 2000: Yahoo! announces 2-for-1 stock split.

◆ April 5, 2000: Yahoo! posts $228 million in revenues, $63 million in pro forma net income.

◆ June 26, 2000: Yahoo! enters the highly competitive business-to-business marketplace with the announcement of Corporate Yahoo!

◆ June 28, 2000: Yahoo! signs agreement to acquire the email group communication service company eGroups.

◆ August 1, 2000: Nielsen//NetRatings' first-ever global Internet index crowns Yahoo! as the top Web property in the world with a unique audience totaling more than 62 million users, representing a stunning reach of 54 percent.

# REFERENCES

McCafferty, Richard (2000) "Yahoo Growing Gangbusters," The Motley Fool, April 6, 2000.

Reeves, Richard, with Caplin, Joan (1997) "25 Years of Money/ Having It All/How to Get Rich: The New Wealth," *Money*, October 1, 1997.

Holt, Mark and Sacoolas, Marc (1995) "... Chief Yahoos: David Filo and Jerry Yang," *What's Happening*, June/July 1995, Sun Microsystems.

Morris, Valerie (1997) "It's Only Money," CNNfn, September 24, 1997.

Williams, Martyn (1995) "Internet's Yahoo Becomes a Full-time Job," Newsbytes News Network, April 20, 1995.

One

# UNDERSTAND THE MEDIUM AND ITS MESSAGE

# SPACE AGE COWBOYS NAVIGATE THE NEW FRONTIER

Writing about one of the pioneering companies of the Internet – or "first movers" as they are more commonly known in netspeak – or, for that matter, writing about the Internet itself, is a little like writing about the Wild West. The only difference is that the journalists who wrote about the Wild West glamorized and invented a lot of what they wrote – hell, they plain lied in many cases – to get and keep their readers' attention. The Internet, on the other hand, is the real deal. No lies are necessary. In fact, the truth is so compelling that it sounds as far-fetched as good science fiction, telling a story of unparalleled growth and extraordinary developments the likes of which most of us living on this planet have never seen, nor ever will again.

Let's start by looking at the Internet population or the number of people using the Internet. Currently, the Internet population is roughly the same as that of the United States. Yet just five years ago, it was about the same as the population of the state of Arizona. Quite impressive. But that's just the beginning.

In another five years the Internet population is projected to rival that of China. Mind you, this figure is controversial. We have to point out that the figures are taken from the numbers of hosts (computer systems with Internet addresses), networks, and domain names with server records. (For a good statistical record of the growth of Internet, its sites, hosts, domains and networks, see the Hobbes' Internet Timeline v.5.0 copyright by Robert Hobbes' Zakon and hosted by the Internet Society [ISOC], Reston, Virginia, at their Web site http://www.isoc.org.) So the number could be much larger or possibly, but not likely, smaller than quoted above.

Where do we go from here? Recently, Joe Connoly of the *Wall Street Journal*, speaking on CBS News Radio, (May 4, 2000) quoted a professional at a venture capital conference as saying the Internet won't stop growing until it is in every car, in every home and in every pocket. And he figures that will take another ten years. So this phenomenon known as the Internet is an epic that has more amazement in store for us than we have yet to see.

**In another five years the Internet population is projected to be the same as that of China.**

Now let's just drop into this mesmerizing setting a couple of wunderkinds – Jerry Yang and David Filo – who were PhD candidates in electrical engineering at Stanford University's grad school. They were one part kid – just having "fun" indexing sites on the Web, and making up directories of all these sites they found on the Internet; one part idea – putting their index of sites up on the Web to make it easier for fellow Internet players to search out stuff; and one part passion – the more they did this, the more they liked it and the less time they spent on their academic pursuits. To quote from Yahoo!'s company history:

"During 1994 they (Filo and Yang) converted Yahoo! into a customized database designed to serve the needs of the thousands of users that began to use the service through the closely bound Internet community. They developed customized software to help them efficiently locate, identify and edit material stored on the Internet."

This was similar to what the venerable book cataloguers used to do in the larger bookstores just a few decades ago. And there you have the makings of a great corporate "wealth-builder" story. Twenty years ago it could have been two kids cataloguing their stamp collection or a book cataloguer indexing texts for a subject-based catalog to be mailed out to the bookstore's customers. Of course, the story would have had a very different ending.

# THE MEDIUM

The difference here between Filo and Yang having fun cataloguing and indexing and some researcher at the corporate library is the medium. Filo and Yang were working with an unprecedented new medium, the Internet. The environment is such a critical part of the story that we have to digress just briefly and take a closer look at what it is.

## What is the Internet?

It is a medium for global connection. What's more:

◆ it is a worldwide network of computers;

◆ it is growing at an exponential rate; and

◆ it has evolved into what is commonly known as the "information superhighway."

Users are primarily the "with-it" generation and prime consumers, from teenagers to middle-aged baby boomers. However, it is changing rapidly. For example, a few years ago, Internet users were mostly male. Now it's about evenly split. In 1997 most Internet users were in the US and UK. Now there are millions of users in South America and Asia. China alone has four developing portals that have recently gone live.

## Why is the Internet such an important phenomenon?

◆ It offers the world universal access and connectivity;

◆ it has democratized a wealth of information; and

◆ its depth and scope is increasing exponentially each year.

## Why is it growing so fast?

Information on the Internet has high value, especially since:

◆ it is updated regularly;

◆ it is interactive;

◆ it is accessible 24/7/365;

◆ it is high speed (Modem, ISDN, Cable TV, DSL, T-l);

◆ users are increasing at the rate of ten percent per month;

◆ it transmits data, voice, audio and video; and

◆ the cost of connection and transmission of data are low and getting less expensive each year, and in some cases the connection is free.

Finally while the Internet was originally a research and then a consumer medium, it is now being adopted by businesses as quickly as it was by consumers. Why?

It offers businesses so many advantages in working with its customers, suppliers and business partners. To name a few:

◆ it is available 24/7/365;

◆ information transfer is faster than mail, FedEx, and even fax;

◆ data are legible and accurate (faxes can be hard to read; handwritten messages often illegible);

◆ information gathering is more timely than most print media (due to cycle-time reduction);

◆ it consumes less resources (paper);

◆ it is less expensive than other media; and

◆ it offers end-to-end commercial business transactions direct to the consumer in real time.

Put it all together and it's not hard to see how the young gunslingers at the Yahoo! Corporation, founded a mere five years ago, are at the head of the space-age cowboys navigating the new frontier. (Fast forward to the present for just a moment; Yahoo! has a $67 billion market capitalization and that's about half of where it's been at the height of the market in 1999.)

At first glance, you'd think that given the Internet tidal wave, which is a once-in-a-lifetime opportunity, the only thing you need for success is just to "be there" when it happens. But that would be an oversimplification. The landscape is already littered with the first-generation casualties of the Internet boom. Many of them have been rescued by takeovers (Netscape, CompuServe) and others will sink without a bubble.

> **The landscape is already littered with the first-generation casualties of the Internet boom.**

## WHAT'S IN A NAME – AN IMAGE AND A BRAND

Yahoo! has had purpose, focus and a consistent identity from its earliest days. The name Yahoo! was no fluke. It was chosen with intent. So why "Yahoo!"?

It's commonly reported that Yahoo! is an anagram for "Yet Another Highly Officious Oracle," but Yang and Filo say they selected the name after looking it up in the dictionary. Tim Koogle commented during an interview that "Jerry and David were looking for a name for the company ... a strong brand. David's father used to refer to him as a yahoo when he was a little boy, back in Louisiana. They looked up the word in the dictionary and found references to an unruly set of ruffians. They thought it described them well, was clever and catchy, and they picked that name." (CNNFn, January 15, 1998) As for the exclamation point, Yang says it was "pure hype."

Fact is, Yahoo! is more than just a name. It has become the signature of a cool place to go on the Web. A cool name for a cool new medium. And it is still the company and portal name today.

> **Fact is, Yahoo! is more than just a name. It has become the signature of a cool place to go on the Web.**

The name was so important that it was even a factor when Yang, Filo and their venture-capital partner, Michael Moritz of Sequoia Capital, were interviewing potential CEOs. They eliminated one candidate solely based on his comment that the first thing he'd do was change the name.

## Modeling for a new advertising medium

While the Internet was burgeoning to become the medium for global connections, Yahoo! was fast becoming one of the few places where a lot of the people who were seeking to get connected would regularly check in. They were becoming a community of users. Consequently, said Jerry Yang, "we had become a medium that could sell advertising." (*Money*, October 1, 1997)

Jerry Yang and David Filo saw Yahoo! as more than just a search engine. It was a medium that could sell advertising to companies or sponsors who wanted to get in front of the eyeballs that searched and studied their directories. This was shrewd thinking. What makes advertisers flock to Yahoo! rather than print is exposure and the fact that Internet users are interactive with the site. No print publication can offer the same dimension and scarcely a whole group of publications worldwide could hope to be seen by the number of people who visit Yahoo! every day.

Yang and Filo had clear and distinct ideas about their vision for Yahoo!

◆ to make it more interactive;

◆ to develop a sense of community; and

◆ to stay free for users.

In 1995, Jerry Yang told *USA Today* reporter Leslie Miller that "we are committed to keeping Yahoo! free for the end-user, while continuing to add enhancements and maintaining our own editorial flavor" (*USA Today*, April 13, 1995). That's still true today.

So far, the Internet tidal wave has been about the consumer; at least the first wave. Consumers who are in love with the Internet have one thing in common. Eyeballs. And who captures the most eyeballs owns the turf. Yahoo!'s Jerry Yang believes his business is about giving users more reasons to return to visit Yahoo! than anywhere else.

If anybody can relate to the Yahoo! user, it is Dave Filo and Jerry Yang. They started in the early days just like the pioneer entrepreneurs you read about in the business success tabloids.

They were camped out in a trailer stocked with workstations from Stanford, living on take-out food and huddled over PCs, while browsing their heads off non-stop to compile a list of favorite Web sites. That's what they called the first list of categorized sites they put up on the Web. Using software they created, Yang and Filo did the job that the first generation of the Mosaic browser couldn't – categorize and subcat- egorize a hit list of Web sites into folders. Like an infohighway Dewey decimal system. The hier- archy they developed made it fairly easy even for neophytes to find what they wanted – and find it quickly. Filo was convinced that "no technology could beat the human filtering" process.

> Filo was convinced that "no technology could beat the human filtering" process.

At the root of it all, Yang and Filo are also convinced they know what the real people who cruise the Internet want and they will give it to them. For free!

## THE NEW MESSAGE: LET THE MEDIUM BE FREE TO THE USER

So many companies have used the free-user business model that it seems very "me-too." The landscape is shotgunned with dot coms that will soon be heading for a black hole in deep space or, if they are lucky, into the arms of bigger brethren with the green fuel to keep going, aka CASH.

At Yahoo! there is a big difference underlying the free-user model. Since they do not have a direct billing relationship with the customer the way an AOL, MSN or AT&T Worldnet has, they must rely on the higher-risk strategy of brand loyalty to bring customers and users back regularly. This may be crazy, but the chief Yahoos! in Santa Clara seem crazy like foxes. Rather than being stuck with a bygone strategy, these bold tacticians are constantly dreaming up new things, new features and new alliances to keep Yahoo! users coming back for more.

## CHARGE ADVERTISERS FOR EXPOSURE

So where's the beef? Or, where does the money come from? From advertising revenue. From year one, Yahoo! has attracted advertisers who want to get in front of their users, and these advertisers are paying real money (not soft dollars or barter but real cash) for banner ad rates that are priced on the per-thousand exposures or eyeballs they get in front of. As early as 1996, advertising was already growing rapidly as marketers were seeking an effective way to reach targeted demographic groups via the Web.

**By fall 1996, Yahoo! was getting nine million plus page views per day.**

And search engines such as Yahoo! were prime attractors of advertising dollars. By fall 1996, Yahoo! was getting over nine million page views per day (Alex Brown & Sons research report by Andrikopoulos).

In the spring of 1997, the Yahoo! Network was developed featuring 30 Web sites, so advertisers could buy space in niche categories. More than Excite or Infoseek, Yahoo! was acting like an interactive media company. The major magazines discovered long ago that while you could charge subscribers at least a nominal amount to receive the magazine every month, it wouldn't pay for paper, printing, shipping, and editorial costs. You need advertisers for that. Yahoo! simply pushed the envelope by not charging subscribers at all. It got all its revenue from advertisers. Yet it did this almost intuitively. But Yang and Filo did so many other things intuitively, like knowing they had to create a brand and hiring the management talent to run things early on.

Also, it didn't hurt that Yang and Filo were toiling during the pioneer days of the Internet in Silicon Valley in a school where so many other technical whizzes congregated.

A golden rule of the new medium is to continuously attract new users. As the company continued its quest to attract more and more new users to its site, it hired Srinija Srinivasan, a Stanford alumna with artificial intelligence expertise, to become the "Ontological Yahoo!" Not a bad thing to be in charge of. Srinivasan oversees the organization of the branching hierarchies that steer people to content. Millions of daily users begin their Web journey by moving through one or more of the key Yahoo! categories: Arts, Business & Economy, Computers & Internet, Education, Entertainment, Government, Health, News & Media, Recreation & Sports, Reference, Regional, Science, Social Science, Society & Culture, and that is just the tip of the iceberg. The rapid growth of the Web has prompted Yahoo! to integrate AltaVista's search engine to provide an ultra-comprehensive directory for "content-based" searches. So far the plan is working, as Yahoo! has become the number-one portal on the Web, and the number-two player in visitor numbers and page views per month.

# GAINING TRUST OF USERS

If there are any secrets to Yahoo!'s success they may lie in how it has executed its plan on all fronts, beginning with the reputation it has gained with users. Paul Noglows, an Internet/digital-media analyst at Hambrecht & Quist, told attendees of the Informed Investors Internet Stocks Forum in 1999 that "Yahoo!, like AOL, has earned the trust of its users." Noglows also listed the eight essential elements he uses to value Internet companies: management, brand, first-mover advantage, venture backing, strategic alliances, business model, international potential and overall market opportunity. He also was emphatic about brand, which we discuss in a later chapter. However, brand develops through the trust that's built with the user. As we will show throughout the book, Yahoo!'s engine has fired on all eight value cylinders in the Internet space.

# DUBBED THE "SWITZERLAND" OF THE INTERNET

Independence may be the riskiest of all bets in the Internet game. However, Yahoo!'s corporate strategists have been successfully playing this high-risk, bet-the-company game for five years now.

Yahoo! is clearly one of the pioneer success stories in the Internet era. Its current position as market leader has largely been due to its triumph as a brand leader on the Web, developing a distinctively different type of intuitive Internet directory, rapid expansion that has kept its competitors at bay, a proven ability to generate profits from advertising, and a fierce determination to stay an independent company. As a result, its market cap is high, and it has a strong currency – its common stock – to use in buying other companies that fit its expansion strategy. The explosive growth of the Internet and Yahoo!'s early-mover status has worked well for the company to date.

However, remaining independent while keeping the corporate promise of being "the only place anyone has to go to get connected to anything or anybody," in the ever-expanding universe of the Web, is a tall order. Right now, nobody in the world has more traffic than Yahoo! does, at least according to Nielsen//NetRatings (for June 2000, they rank Yahoo! #1 globally with a unique audience of 62,772,590 visitors. In the US, Yahoo! ranks #3 at 49,045,000 as of July 2000, right behind the other two Internet titans, AOL and Microsoft).

Along with providing services free to users, the company chooses to remain neutral toward content providers and devices regarding ownership of its content. In contrast, AOL's recent merger with Time Warner will bind it to content and cable subscribers of Time Warner. AT&T has placed its bets on cable with the purchase of Excite@Home. At press time, Lycos is about to merge with Tera Networks in a $12 billion dollar deal, which has the giant German media company Bertlesmann purchasing $1 billion in advertising and services, and providing content. Yahoo!'s strategy has been to ally with as many partners as possible – both big and small – and promote them to its user base. According to analysts the Lycos deal was "inevitable" given its fading position compared with market leaders Yahoo!, AOL, and MSN. "They have pretty much created a glass ceiling for other general interest portals." (CNET News.com, May 16, 2000)

## Consolidating and integrating

The shakeout in portals started in 1999 with the purchase of Excite by @Home, and CMGI's majority-owned AltaVista stepping back to focus on a narrower search-engine strategy. Disney's Go.com has recast itself as an entertainment site.

For Yahoo! so far so good. So long as user loyalty remains high and it keeps delivering on its promises. Of course, Yahoo! has rapidly expanded its footprint in the services space by purchasing a string of service companies such as Four11 Corporation, in October 1997, a privately held online communications and Internet white pages directory; Viaweb, June 10, 1998, a provider of software and services for hosting online stores; WebCal, on July 17, 1998, a privately-held developer and marketer of Web-based calendaring and scheduling products, and publisher of EventCal, a comprehensive database of worldwide public events; Yoyodyne Entertainment, Inc., October 20, 1998, a privately-held direct marketing services company; Hyperparallel, Inc. on December 17, 1998, a direct marketing company specializing in data analysis; GeoCities on January 28, 1999, a publicly traded Internet company; and Broadcast.com on July 20, 1999, which offers streaming video. The future may lie in how many other smart deals they can put together. "If they continue cutting good deals, it could have a huge payoff," according to Charlene Li of Forrester Research.

Meanwhile as the remaining portals play the bulking up services game, Yahoo! and AOL have emerged as the leaders in the game of partnering, adding services, and buying up smaller companies that's consolidating the winners into a precious few. According to Emily Meehan at the Internet market research firm Yankee Group, "the reality is that AOL and Yahoo are far and away the No. 1 players here, and it will take quite a bit for another silver medalist to slide up next to AOL." (CNET News.com, May 16, 2000.)

Arm in arm with the good deals Yahoo! has put together, is its skill at integration. The company seems to be exceptionally good at managing the properties it has acquired. The challenge for the future is to keep expanding while continuing to manage everything under one roof, according to Kathey Hale of Gartner Group. She specifically cites Yahoo!'s push into the small business area by launching its business-to-business marketplace in March 2000. This targets a different business group than the one that took them to the dance in the first place. "I almost sense that they've been conflicted on direction … (valuing) independence so high they're being undermined by uncertainty." (Knight Ridder Newspapers, April 17, 2000.)

> "We have a strong belief about where the Internet is going and have to make sure we don't rest on our laurels. It's not about how big you are but how fast you are.
> **– Jerry Yang**

To Yang it is still early in the game. "We have a strong belief about where the Internet is going and have to make sure we don't rest on our laurels. It's not about how big you are but how fast you are. We are paranoid about what we need to do next." (Knight Ridder Newspapers, April 17, 2000.) Andy Grove would be proud.

The only way for Yahoo! to stay on top of their game is to be faster, smarter and quicker than the next gunslingers coming down the street looking to prove themselves better or faster than Yahoo! itself. To help everybody keep their eye on the

ball, and remind them there is no time to stop and rest, Yang
has another translation of the Yahoo! logo: "You always have
other options."

# HOW TO BE THE NEXT
# TOP GUNSLINGER

◆ *Stay at the top of your game.* Often the difference between the
first and second place in cyberspace is not just how good
you are but how good you can stay.

◆ *Know who your enemies are.* The competition is very predatory
in Internet land. As Tim Koogle told Mary Meeker and Bill
Gurley at the Internet Summit in California in July 2000,
"the company isn't too specific about ... plans." If you have
something big up your sleeve, keep quiet about it until you're
ready to go.

◆ *Shoot first, aim second.* You can't afford to be second. The
sureshot may cost you the opportunity. You might be dead
already. You need to arrive early to get the best position.

# REFERENCES

CBS News Radio, New York City affiliate, Thursday, May 4,
2000.

CNNFn, (1998) Interview with Jan Hopkins on the *Capital
Ideas* program, January 15, 1998.

*Money*, October 1, 1997.

Miller, Leslie (1995) *USA Today*, "Yahoo/The Homespun Web Map," April 13, 1995.

Jim Hu, (2000) CNET News.com, May 16, 2000.

Kristi Heim, (2000) Knight Ridder Newspapers, April 17, 2000.

Two

# PEOPLE OVER TECHNOLOGY, COMMUNITY OVER COMPUTERS

Internet venture capital deals in the first five months
of 2000 totaled over $28 billion
**– internet.com**

# IT'S NOT ABOUT THE TECHNOLOGY STUPID; IT'S THE PERSONAL TOUCH

There are hundreds of millions of pages of content available on the Web, and it's growing at triple-digit rates yearly. So how do the online media moguls at Yahoo! maintain their lead in this hot-growth, technology-based medium called the Internet?

By serving as human guides to the information superhighway. It's not about the technology, not here. Yahoo!'s search engine is neither the fastest nor arguably even the best – a fact most portal visitors would probably dispute. Yet the perception is that Yahoo! is the best. A few years ago even Tim Koogle thought so. The CEO was caught by surprise once at an industry conference when a competitor bragged about how his company searches were seconds faster than Yahoo!'s. As soon as he was able, he caught up with Jerry Yang and asked, "Is that true?" (*Fortune*, March 2 1998). Of course, it was. Yang knew this to be true, but he didn't care that much. Koogle eventually came to learn why. Fact is, speediest or not, more people go to Yahoo! every month than go to AOL or any other portal because lovers of the Internet may not be the technophiles who started it. More and more, it's the millions of new users who get on the Internet each year and keep coming back to a site. It's mind share. And it thrives on the human touch.

The war of the search engines – now turned to portals – is not about the speed race. It's about winning the hearts and minds of Internet users – the mind share as it's more commonly known – winning over competitors such as Lycos, Excite, Infoseek, and AOL to name a few.

## HOW DOES YAHOO! DO IT?

It starts at the top with Yang, Filo, Mallet and Koogle. They seem to have an innate sense of the Internet being a medium for people to connect – globally – 24/7. The human touch goes back to the earliest days of the company. Filo had it in his gut very early on that Yahoo! could ultimately be a common interface to the Web rather than simply a directory, a search engine or a cool piece of technology (*Fortune* March 6, 2000).

**The war of the search engines – now turned to portals – is not about the speed race. It's about winning the hearts and minds of Internet users ...**

According to Tim Koogle, the company spends its days trying to figure out how to satisfy user needs. That's quite a creed to live up to, given how fast things change on the Web. Beneath it all, there is a set of operating values at work – all aimed at making the site so people-friendly that users will want to stay around. Call it the human touch. At Yahoo!, being people focused is a core competency. And it works.

## VALUE PROPOSITION #1: PEOPLE POWER

Humans attracting lots of other humans with useful information researched, assembled, and categorized by humans. Clearly the company has cultivated a non techno-nerd image.

Yahoo! offers a comprehensive, intuitive and user-friendly online guide to Web navigation, aggregated information content, communications services, a strong user community, and commerce. It includes a hierarchical, subject-based directory of Web sites that enables Web users to locate and access desired information and services through hypertext links included in the directory.

Among the top five success factors in the Internet space are technology and customer-relationship management (CRM). Key to high scoring in CRM is user-friendly interaction and customer service. You can have the zoomiest technology like, say, Excite or Northern Lights or Google, and still not connect with as many people. (Yahoo! did switch its search engine over to Google in the spring of 2000. But this was just icing on the cake.) By keeping it simple and keeping it friendly to humans, the company has kept the site-seers coming.

Mostly it boils down to reaching out to the customer. A few new-economy types understand this, like Mike Pusateri, head of Internet sales and marketing for Marriott International. He is one of the savvy non-technology execs who caught on early to the real significance of the Internet. He knew the value of drawing in customers. "The Internet is all about service – providing service to customers in a way that is faster, friendlier, and more personal than they or the company has ever experienced before. And service is Marriott's business. We don't even own the bricks and mortar in most of our properties." (Bill Gates, *Business At The Speed of Thought.*)

# VALUE PROPOSITION #2:
# CONTENT POWER

The other part of Yahoo!'s proposition is its incorporation of a rich set of current and reference information from leading content providers, including real-time news provided by numerous sources including Reuters New Media, Associated Press, Deutsche Presse Agenture, and Agence France Presse, stock quotes (Reuters), corporate earnings reports (Zacks), audio news (National Public Radio), mutual fund holding (CDA/Wiesenberger), financial reporting (Forbes.com, The Street.com, The Motley Fool), sports scores (ESPN sports ticker), sports commentary (the *Sporting News*), employment (Wall Street Journal) weather information (Weathernews, Inc., and the Weather Channel), and entertainment industry gossip (E! Online). Yahoo! also organizes hypertext links to Web sites featuring current events and issues of interest – such as elections, holidays, political issues and major weather conditions – organized in a topical format and updated regularly. Their current offerings include auctions, Yellow Pages, maps, driving directions, and classifieds listings.

Yahoo! has become a leading communications hub on the Internet. Through its interactive chat service, pages, and message boards, Yahoo! members can contact each other as well as communicate with the Web community at large. Yahoo! has built a community of members who register with the company, and it currently provides more than a dozen registered services for its members including Yahoo! Shopping, Yahoo! Auctions, Yahoo! Clubs, Yahoo! Address Book, Yahoo! Calendar, Yahoo! Mail, Yahoo! Pager, Yahoo! Chat, Yahoo! Message Boards, Yahoo! To Do List.

# VALUE PROPOSITION #3: B2B POWER

In addition, the company has a B2B strategy to provide a marketplace for commerce on the Web. Through alliances with premier merchants, Yahoo! offers its members the opportunity to purchase goods and services, such as books (Amazon.com), music (CDNow), automotive services (Microsoft CarPoint and Autoweb), mortgages (E-Loan), brokerages services (E*Trade, Discover), traditional communications services (AT&T), unified messaging (JFAX), electronics (Value America), sports (Genesis Direct), and magazine subscriptions (Electronic Newsstand). And with the acquisition of Viaweb, it provides a complete service for merchants wishing to reach Yahoo!'s millions of individual users. (Form 10K Annual Report December 31, 1998, p. 3.)

# PEOPLE FOCUS AT THE HOME PAGE

There are a couple of ways aggregators can gather the content on their Web site. One is the use of full text-search engines that use a set of automated methods to point people in the right direction. The user comes into a site, types in a word or phrase – a more advanced user types a string of words with certain qualifiers (known as a Boolean search) – and clicks on the search tab. The engine then goes out and searches a compressed index of text documents that have been selected by a crawler – a robot software program that gathers information on sites all over the Web. It's a little like starting to pour subject matter into the top of a giant funnel with different sized filters. You have to start chugging the information around, narrow down the focus, and eventually get to just the right sites that fit your description.

Yahoo!'s solution: start with a comprehensive directory of sites arranged in a hierarchy based on a number of subjects or themes.

In December 1998, Yahoo! organized well over 1,200,000 Web site listings under the following 14 principal categories: Arts & Humanities, Business & Economy, Computers & Internet, Education, Entertainment, Government, Health, News and Media, Recreation and Sports, Reference, Regional, Science, Social Science, and Society & Culture. Web sites are further organized under these major headings by hierarchical subcategories. Users can either directly browse the listings by subject matter, or use a rapid keyword search facility that scans the contents of the entire directory or any subcategory within Yahoo! The basic Web-site listings are in many cases supplemented with brief descriptive commentary, and a special symbol is used to indicate listings that, in the view of the company's editorial staff, provide unique presentation or content within their topic area. Yahoo! also provides Web-wide text search results from the Google search engine. These results are integrated into the directory search function so that Web-wide search results are presented in the absence of relevant listings from the Yahoo! directory. So the reader isn't just limited to the wisdom of the editorial staff – this wisdom is augmented by the more sophisticated technology of an automated search engine. Within each of the subjects or themes there is a breakdown of sites in the style of the table of contents in a book. This allows the users to cruise the already organized table of contents and pick whichever sites may be of interest. It's a way of starting further down the funnel. Obviously, building a site like this takes a lot of editors. So at Yahoo! you'll find a lot more people at work sorting and categorizing sites than you will at the bot shops.

# KEEP IT SIMPLE, KEEP IT FRIENDLY, KEEP 'EM COMING

So how do the technologists get to the people? By putting people first and technology second. Sounds a little wacky for a high-tech company. Well, maybe.

What's the thinking behind the practice? Given Yahoo!'s roots, the angle seems to be: keep it simple and friendly to humans. It's just that simple. And given the number of unique visitors to the site on the Web, maybe we should add: keep them coming!

## Why keep it simple?

Whatever the strategic platform, the company founders seem to know what the people want. From the beginning and right up until the present, the Yahoo! site has a less complex look and feel to it, and a lot less graphics, than many other portals.

The reality of the Internet is that not everyone has the latest and greatest multimedia, multitasking, high-megahertz, high-bandwidth box at their command. So Yahoo!'s information pages come up quickly without a lot of bells and whistles. Translation: It loads fast. It's like a good old-fashioned welcome mat. Plain, simple and inviting. At competitor sites – some at least – you'll find row upon row of servers and workstations. Yahoo!'s hardware operation is outsourced. At company HQ, you'll find mostly people in cubicles and a couple of black

> ... Yahoo!'s information pages come up quickly without a lot of bells and whistles.

boxes, not farms of servers. By connecting the human touch with cool amenities and free features like stock quotes, maps, free email, customizable My Yahoo! pages, classifieds, auctions, "Yellow Pages" and more, "it looks and feels more like an online service. (*Fortune*, March 2, 1998 p.14.)

---

When considering how much technology to apply when designing your site and its Web pages, ask yourself these questions, before a competitor does:

◆ *What attracts people to a site?* Its ease of use, simplicity, non-tech lingo (except, of course for the numerous sites targeted to tech professionals), convenience and service.

◆ *How does your site plan measure up in each of these areas?* Visit competitor sites both for ideas and benchmarks for your platform. And remember, if you want to attract an android or propeller head, go with in-your-face technology and futuristic screen dazzlers. If you want to bring in the people, drop the bells and whistles, except for the transparent ones, and stick with a simple, clean, friendly, basic look.

◆ *What attracts users to the site?*

◆ *How fast can users get to the information they seek?*

◆ *How quickly can they get something done?* Whether it be searches, links, directions or transactions, consider the completion time. How many of us have abandoned sites in the middle of a purchase or a permission-marketing transaction because of annoyingly long sequences needed to get the thing we wanted accomplished?

In a few years, when more than 70 percent of people can access the Web and browse via mobile wireless devices, with their very small screens, graphics-rich and other complex sites will have an even tougher time keeping consumers interested in coming back regularly.

# HIERARCHIES HANDCRAFTED BY PEOPLE

Robert Reid, in his 1997 book, *The Architects of the Web*, noted that the Yahoo! "hierarchy is a handcrafted tool ... people designated the categories, not computers. The sites that they link to are likewise deliberately chosen, not assigned by software algorithms. In other words, this online media company has editors making judgment calls, just like the old-fashioned media giants.

"Clearly, Yahoo! is a very labor intensive product. But it is also a guide with human discretion and judgment built into it – and this can at times make it almost uncannily effective ... This is the essence of Yahoo!'s uniqueness and (okay, let's say it) genius. It isn't especially interesting to point to information that many people are known to find interesting, *TVGuide* does this. So do phone books, and countless Web sites that cater to well-defined interest groups ... But Yahoo! is able to build intuitive paths that might be singularly, or even temporarily important to the people seeking it. And it does this in a way that no other service has truly replicated."

## Make it easy for the user to get connected

Another principle behind the Yahoo! story is its single-minded focus on the consumer, the user of the site. It was one of the reasons why in January 1998 Yahoo! struck an alliance with MCI Communications (now WorldCom) to offer Yahoo! Online powered by MCI Internet. The new service was aimed at the first-time Internet user. As Jeff Mallet told reporters, the service was the easiest way to link up to the Internet, and it was designed "to give the new user the best and easiest service for getting connected to the Internet."

As the Web becomes more a part of mainstream culture, Yahoo! continues to grow and change. In 1998 it had already begun its transformation from a search engine with human editors to a worldwide media portal. Today the company describes its *raison d'être* as the "only place anyone has to go to get connected to anything or anybody. This concept is appealing to people, and I believe that is a key reason why Yahoo! is part of the lives of so many people." (Yahoo! Annual Report, 1998.)

**"If you want to catch a mouse, make a noise like a cheese."**
**– Charles Tandy**

## GUIDING PRINCIPLES FOR PEOPLE-CATCHING ON THE WEB

*Cultivate a non-techno-nerd image.* Yahoo! went with the maverick funloving approach to people. They projected their grassroots image – two guys fooling around with a personal passion that erupted into a full-time business. Quite a different story from the rest of the Silicon Valley contenders. Other populist approaches that have similarly bred success: The Motley Fool was founded in 1993 by brothers David and Tom Gardner who donned jester hats to shrewdly promote their beliefs that there isn't all that much mystery to this complicated-sounding financial stuff, and that any individual investor can do it with the right motivation and information. All of this brought to you by a couple of guys who are – like the court jesters of medieval times – able to tell the simple truth and get away with it. In the investing field they are most similar to Yahoo! in cultivating a friendly image. Borrowing directly from their site:

"We exist to serve you, to teach you, and to have a heck of a lot of fun along the way. We believe that:

1. You are the most capable person alive to manage your money.
2. This stuff isn't rocket science; we all just need to learn together.
3. Being smart about your money can be a lot of fun ... really!
4. You can make a fortune doing it."

*Reach out to customers.* Provide services users want and need. "Services," according to Carly Fiorina, CEO of Hewlett Packard, "drive the customer experience." And he who gives the customer the best experience will get them back again and again. The more services you provide, the more users will have a reason to visit your site. Yahoo! continually adds services that make it more user-friendly and comfortable for users to hang around. The latest Nielsen//NetRatings confirm that the average user-time spent on its sites is the highest in the world. Even the automobile is now being recognized as an electronic communications platform that can reach out with services to the consumer. For instance, the On Star Navigation system from General Motors allows you to punch in a request for alternative routes right from your car whenever you are in a traffic jam.

*Keep the portal simple.* Nothing wears out faster than fancy pages that take forever to load. Graphics are neat but simple is sublime. Even with increased broadband capabilities, it's going to take quite a while for broadband's reach to extend to most of the people on the Web. In the meantime think about what most of the people out there are using to get on the Web. Richard Prentice Ettinger who founded one of the early large publishing empires, Prentice-Hall (now a part of Pearson PLC), used to say: "Think like the birds think." And Charles Tandy, founder of the consumer electronics chain Radio Shack, puts it this way: "If you want to catch a mouse, make a noise like a cheese." Given that most people will not have state-of-the-art computers or the latest and greatest bandwidth, keep it simple.

# REFERENCES

Stross, Randall E. (1998) "How Yahoo! Won the Search Wars" *Fortune*, March 2 1998, p. 148ff.

Schendler, Brent (2000) "The Capitalist Century, How a Virtuoso plays the Web Electric," *Fortune* March 6, 2000, p. F79.

Gates, Bill (1999) *Business At The Speed of Thought*, Warner Books, 1999, p. 102.

*Fortune*, March 2, 1998, pp. 14.

Koogle, Tim (1998) Letter to Shareholders, 1998 Annual Report, p.13.

Three

# BUILD LOCAL COMMUNITIES IN THE GLOBAL VILLAGE

C ommunity building is a key plank in portal-building strategy. It helps bring in new people, keeps them on the site and generally develops user loyalty. While it is probably not a place for advertisers to focus excessively, it is certainly a way for marketers to selectively target key demographics and psychographics for their products and services (Newsbytes News Network, August 18, 1998). Yahoo!'s vision of community has a global dimension to it, but it also has certain communities of interest within it.

## THINK GLOBAL ACT LOCAL – METROPOLITAN YAHOO!S

The first plank in Yahoo!'s global community platform was the creation of local sites beginning with Yahoo! San Francisco Bay area in June 1996. Like the other vertical sites that followed, it included everything from local directories in ten categories ranging from business to education, employment, recreation, entertainment and travel as well as chamber-of-commerce type tourist information, local sports, driving directions, Yellow Pages, an online community section and community news. As the vertical metropolitan site model developed, it was expanded to other major metro area locations. First Los Angeles, then New York, followed by Atlanta, Boston, Dallas/Fort Worth, Chicago, and Washington, DC. Then Yahoo! began developing local sites for all 50 states.

# EXPAND THE PLATFORM GLOBALLY
# BUT KEEP THE LOCAL FLAVOR

Expansion of the global platform was clearly on the founders' radar screen, and that vision was blessed by good fortune. A hundred million dollars' worth. Yahoo!'s main early investor, aside from Sequoia Partners, was Softbank – the multi-billion dollar software and media company – run by its founder, the international wheeler-dealer Masayoshi Son, who had just concluded purchasing the Ziff Davis company in 1995.

Son spent many years in San Francisco, went to school at the University of California at Berkeley, studied computers, and made his first million by selling a translator to the Sharp Corporation and importing video games. He then returned to Japan to start Softbank. Clearly, Son was a maverick in his own right. He certainly fell foul of the Japanese business and banking mainstream, when he purchased Comdex early in 1995 without getting permission from his main bank investor, the Industrial Bank of Japan. A fallout ensued, and it would have been disastrous had it not been for last-minute new backing Son got from Nomura Securities. They were going to say no but were put under a lot of pressure from Japan's Foreign Ministry to provide the necessary funding. According to press accounts, being an outcast in the clubby, traditional Japanese business world, along with his West Coast American business exposure, probably made Son more open to new ideas.

Right after purchasing the Ziff Davis publications in 1995, Son stopped by to see its CEO, Eric Hippeau. During the meeting Son asked him to name the one Internet outfit to invest in. Hippeau replied "Yahoo!" Son immediately approached the young company, less than a year old, with hardly any employees and losing money (but not much by Internet standards).

After several back-and-forths between Son and a very reluctant Yahoo! – fearful that Son would try and change their culture to a Japanese-style company – Son finally convinced company officials to take the $100 million he had earmarked to invest in the Internet, a business he felt he "had to be in." According to a report in the *Washington Post*, it was either going to be with Yahoo!, a competitor of theirs, or Son might just have to start a company himself (*Washington Post*, May 9, 1999).

Wisdom prevailed and Yahoo! okayed Softbank's purchase of about a one-third stake in the company.

> **Yahoo! was more concerned with growth, with capitalizing on its assets and amassing more eyeballs, than it was with being gobbled up by partners with deep pockets.**

You get a different and highly plausible spin on how developments played out if you read the incisive chapter on Tim Koogle that appears in the book *Champions of Silicon Valley* (Wiley, 2000) by Charles G. Sigismund. He talked with the CEO on a number of occasions between October 1997 and spring 1998, a time when Yahoo! was rapidly developing. Koogle said that Yahoo! already had a developing content arrangement with Ziff – as it did with Reuters – and realizing that Yahoo!'s valuations were going up, he set out to put together a number of "strategic partnerships" where companies would become investors. This made sense, as the company had no intention of competing with monster original content providers.

Naturally there was paranoia in the air and Koogle dealt with it by developing relationships with both Eric Hippeau of Ziff Davis and Masayoshsi Son of Softbank, as well as the head of Reuters. Yahoo! was more concerned with growth, with capitalizing on its assets and amassing more eyeballs, than it was with being gobbled up by partners with deep pockets. It was also very risk-oriented. Koogle felt it was worth expanding into markets outside the US, even at the risk of spreading itself too thinly. The reward side of the coin was compelling. By getting in very early, if successful, Yahoo! would create high entry barriers for any that followed and establish a strong market position for itself as a first mover.

Soon afterward, Yahoo! launched its first geographic property. Company documents state that Yahoo! Japan Corporation was formed with Softbank (a 36 percent owner in Yahoo! at that point) to establish and manage, in Japan, a Japanese version of the Yahoo! Internet Guide, develop related Japanese online navigational services, and conduct other related business. Yahoo! Japan launched on April 1, 1996 and neither Yahoo! nor Softbank has had any reason to look back since.

Partnering with Ziff and Softbank was the key to global expansion for Yahoo!, first in Japan, and then in Europe and the UK. As Koogle tells it: "We sat down with Son and said, 'You know we want you as an investor to help us capitalize this company, but the business relationship also means leverage in international markets.'" He also thought "maybe if we structure this thing right with Softbank, we can go and launch properties in other parts of the world, in partnership with (Softbank). Make use of their infrastructure. Not have to invest in that. When we invest, we invest light, but we invest in the people who are actually adding value from day one." (*Champions of Silicon Valley*, p. 123.)

Yahoo! Japan was an instant success, becoming the most popular site in Japan, and it was profitable in its second month. In 1997 it went public. So successful was the venture that by June 2000 Jean-Pascal Rolandez, a securities analyst heading up research at BNP Paribas Group in Tokyo, told *Business Week* reporter Ben Belson: "Yahoo! Japan has blown away local competitors such as Sony's So-net and phone giant Nippon Telegraph and Telephone's Goo." Belson further declared, they are "virtually alone."

While other international sites have been launched, it's likely that Yahoo! Japan will continue to lead the pack with an estimated 85 percent of local Net users visiting the site each month and advertising revenue growth that outstrips the US site.

Call it shrewd or call it lucky. By linking back to US sites on each of the category pages in Yahoo! Japan, the overseas site drove increased traffic to the US with its all-English pages. The parent company's initial investment in the venture was $729,000. By spring 2000, Yahoo! Japan was the first publicly held Japanese company whose shares were trading at a market capitalization of above 100 million yen.

# BORROW THE BEST IDEAS, LEVERAGE RELATIONSHIPS AND KEEP THE TIES THAT BIND

Aside from moving fast, there are two critical reasons why Yahoo! Japan trumped its rivals: first it had an exchange deal with its US cousin allowing full adaptation of whatever it wanted from the US site in return for a three percent cut of revenue;

second, and just as important, was the largesse of Softbank – a 51 percent owner of Yahoo! Japan – which provided both content and advertising to Yahoo! Japan from its myriad Web ventures. Imitating its success and capitalizing on its relationship with Softbank proved an unbeatable combination.

**Yahoo! Japan was an instant success, becoming the most popular site in Japan, and it was profitable in its second month.**

Perhaps the unheralded capstone to the success story of Yahoo! Japan is the fact that there is no comparable Nipponese version of either AOL or Microsoft in existence. Yahoo! was smart enough to realize it had to move early to grab position ahead of the competition that was certain to follow.

## CAPITALIZE ON SUCCESS BY CLONING IT – AND NEVER LOOK BACK
### Yahoo! Europe

Both the company and Softbank clearly realized the importance of being early and building momentum. To expand the international property, the 1997 financials indicate they formed a joint venture agreement on November 1, 1996, establishing Yahoo! Europe and further creating separate companies in Germany, the United Kingdom, and France to establish and manage versions of the Yahoo! Internet Guide for each country. Unlike the Japan site, this time Yahoo! retained the majority interest in the expansion sites. Not all of the sibling sites are as full featured as their parent. In France, for example, there were special government regulations that prevented the Auctions feature from being implemented until several years later.

Smart customization of the portals in local languages, bolstered the company brand name both internationally and locally. And the turf game continued on additional fronts.

## Yahoo! Korea

In August 1997, Yahoo! signed a joint venture agreement with Softbank and affiliate companies to form Yahoo! Korea, another local version of the Internet Guide, plus develop related Korean online navigational services.

## Yahoo! China

Expanding in Asia is key to the company's global strategy, but some areas are more difficult than others. Although Jerry Yang is no stranger to Asia, being the son of Chinese parents born in Taiwan, China has maintained a policy of not allowing foreign investment in Internet service and content providers. However, with the opening of China's doors to obtain membership of the World Trade Organization, there's probably a future Yahoo! China site on the cards. In May 1998, Yahoo! put up Yahoo! Chinese, a search engine with both traditional and simplified Chinese language options that would serve as a vernacular gateway to the Internet. This was mirrored by a similar venture by AltaVista. Then, in September 1999, Yahoo! opened another door into China – if only a little – by starting Yahoo! China, an Internet portal for mainland China, based in Hong Kong. Plans are to move the operation to Beijing.

Yahoo!'s approach to China is to start a dialog with the government. As Heather Killen, vice president of international operations at Yahoo! told a *Dallas Morning News* reporter, "You go there and try to make friends and show a little respect." (*Dallas Morning News*, November 22, 1999) Other reasons for China's reluctance to drop its policies are the lack of electronic commerce capabilities and protection of minors from "unhealthy" content, said Chang Xiaobing, deputy director-general of the telecom bureau in China's Ministry of Information. The key to entry, Xiaobing told a panel of international businessmen, is not by pushing deregulation but "introducing good experiences." (*Dallas Morning News*, November 22, 1999)

Yahoo! intends to extend and expand its international push. Jeff Mallet told a *Minneapolis Star Tribune* reporter (*Minneapolis Star Tribune*, May 30, 1999) that in five years, half a billion people will be online. Most won't be American. So Yahoo! and every other leading Web company is expanding in Europe, Asia and Latin America as quickly as possible. The name of the game is locking in dominant market position, and nobody has the lead for long.

Bruce Klassen, a B2B commerce expert, author, and principal at A.T. Kearney, recently said that first-mover advantage now gives you only about a 90-day lead. So for leaders like Yahoo!, standing pat is never an option.

Appropriately, after only five years Yahoo!'s business vision has gone from being a directory of Internet sites to a search engine, to a media company, to "creating a global comprehensive branded network ... attracting and retaining as large a global audience as possible and giving consumers a singe, trusted and comprehensive place to go for all of their daily needs, be it content, things to buy, or ways to communicate with each other." This mandate requires an aggressive expansionist posture, continued heavy investment in market share and a consistent record of meeting – if not beating – expectations. So far so good.

To date, Yahoo! has grown to meet its visionary expansion plans. But it has also increased its depth by what Koogle calls super-aggregating content and then adding to it live feeds, summary news, and other things associated with the site.

# FOUR WAYS TO BUILD COMMUNITY ON THE WEB

Building communities on the Web is one of the key ways portals have of increasing visitors and keeping them coming back for repeat visits, from which a measure known as "stickiness" is derived. Stickiness is critical in the Web community because customer retention can increase or decrease in a very short time. As a metric, stickiness usually means the average time a visitor spends at the site. It's a more meaningful measure of site performance than page views or unique visitors, according to Tiger Buford, E-Business manager at Avery Dennison. "Successful sites like Yahoo! have both high traffic numbers and high stickiness numbers. Both of these traits are needed for success." Why? Because "high traffic means nothing if a visitor simply clicks through your site to get to another. And stickiness means nothing if your site only gets ten hits a day." Buford lists four important elements of Web-site communities:

1. *Email discussion lists.* These are generally a kind of free-form democratic type of community with very little maintenance or control required. They are driven by automated email systems that allow everyone to subscribe/unsubscribe. And any subscriber can send a message to a single email address that is automatically forwarded

to all of the other subscribers to a particular list. These lists can grow like a virus or die from lack of participation. All thrive by word of mouth. Some broadcast each message as it appears. Others bundle the messages until a certain number collect, and some broadcast a digest of messages at specific intervals. The only downside is their chaotic nature. Also time-zone differences can make it hard to make sense out of responses to previous messages. An example of this is the Yahoo! Finance message boards. Yahoo! does not moderate the lists, so some are very good whilst others are simply rant-and-rave boards or fields for pump-and-dump operators to tout penny stocks nobody ever heard of. That's the nature of the democratic free-form community.

2. *Bulletin boards.* Much like email discussion lists, only more organized. Visitors go to a specific Web site to participate on the bulletin board. Each subject is built upon, so those visitors can chronologically read a discussion of a previous email in a thread. The only drawback is that keeping up with the discussion requires regular visits to the site.

3. *Chat rooms.* Here we find "live" discussions on any number of topics. Chat rooms have become so popular that a new set of protocols – like Robert's Rules of Order – have been developed so the flow of discussion is moderated. Chat rooms can be a boom or a bust depending upon the site. Some sites host celebrities or subject matter experts to draw traffic to their sites. The biggest drawback of chat rooms is that you have to have several people online and actively involved in posting chat at the same time for it to be a draw. Many people just hang out and read the dialog but do not add to the discussion. Buford says chat rooms are the least effective way of building community. Instead, he favors bulletin boards and email discussion lists.

4. *Email newsletters.* Another way to build traffic is the email newsletter that is sent out to lists of subscribing members. Members have to opt in by providing names, emails, addresses, and sometimes

> responses to a few other relevant questions to be accepted. It
> is usually interactive and contains links to sites, questions from
> readers and a feedback to the editor feature. All of this encourages
> member participation although this is the least interactive of the
> community-building methods mentioned above. Yahoo! does not
> have a general email newsletter, but many marketing and media
> organizations (AT&T and MSN for instance) do.

## MARKET RESEARCH – REAL TIME

Taking a cue from The WELL, Web leaders are rushing to
engage their users in hundreds of targeted electronic subcul-
tures by cultivating or acquiring communities appealing to a
sweeping range of tastes and interests.

Yahoo! uses market research and other key strategies in conducting and analyzing results to help it make the right decisions in
building Internet communities. Digital market strategy is largely
developed with the help of tracking software that analyzes what
a user/customer does from the moment he or she opens up the
site. Clickstreams tell the company where the user has been,
and how often and how long they stayed there.

On the Web, market research matters perhaps even more than
ever. With every click on the computer a traceable and trackable
event, leading companies are literally taking the temperature
of the patient – the user of their properties – in real time.
In describing Yahoo!'s properties Koogle has said: "Products
morph on short cycles here ... we put something out there and
look nightly at whether people like it or not and then change it
on that basis" (Sigismund, p.128). In the vertical sites, Yahoo!
watches consumption carefully and then continues to provide

more vertical material. It uses the information on what the masses of users are doing as a window into its universe – almost like in the film *The Truman Show* – watching what the collective minds are doing. From that it can tell what's working and where people are going on its site. From there it plans and organizes extensions and expansion in a very natural way.

To accelerate growth as quickly as possible there's a continual push for add-ons to increase connection time. The more connection that's involved in a site the longer the user stays on. By bringing in as much content and offering added services you keep the user at the site for longer periods of time.

In the summer of 1998, Yahoo! launched its community effort with Yahoo! Clubs. As described by the company, Yahoo! Clubs – again, a free service to users – provided "a unique web address

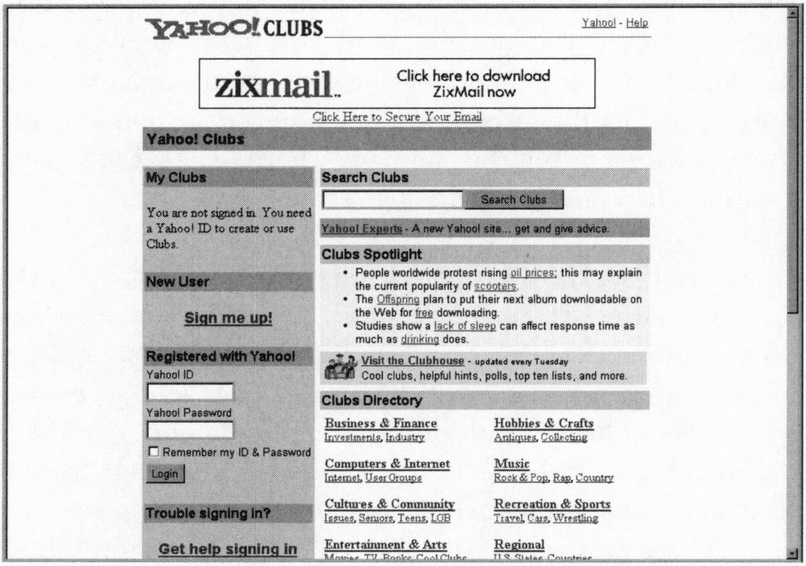

Fig. I    The Yahoo! Clubs home page

and centralized web communications center for groups to develop relationships and interact on a regular basis with friends, relatives and co-workers, and others who share similar interests."

Clubs' target was deliberately broad – workgroups, B2B organizations, families, investment clubs, associations, fan clubs and alumni groups to name a few. No special software or tech skills required. Just choose a category, state whether you want it listed or not, and your are in. Included are founders' tools and features, along with hints on how to create the club, post messages and photos. Clubs was configured with a full-featured platform including message boards, chat rooms, photo albums, email, Web links and a club activity tracker.

# KEY DRIVERS OF COMMUNITY ON THE WEB

When Howard Rheingold, author of *The Virtual Community* (1993, HarperCollins), first wrote about the promise of community and its powerful marketing pull, he felt that warm supportive networks could actually be developed among people who had never met face to face. And although virtual community seems like a contradiction in terms, many innovators have been striving to make community real, since Rheingold's book first appeared.

The first communities on the Web were among scientific researchers who used the Internet to share information, gather research and exchange messages. One of the oldest and best known of these is The WELL, founded in 1985 in the San Francisco area. According to Gail Ann Williams, "the concept of virtual community has gone from something people couldn't believe existed to being the 'killer app' for a profitable Web site. It's the latest gold rush on the Net." True to its non-commercial roots as a group of high-tech enthusiasts and professionals where you could go and ask for information on a specific topic and get help from other members, the WELL hasn't grown anywhere near as fast as the Internet. Nor does it wish to. Staffed primarily by less than a dozen full-time people, it does very little marketing and is a breakeven operation. It has not only fostered community but, according to company officials, it has resulted in friendships off-line. It stays in business by charging members/users a monthly fee and while it doesn't get heavily involved in commerce it does feature and sell books by author/members. It merged with Salon.com in 1998.

## *WHERE THERE IS COMMUNITY, THERE IS COMMERCE*

Of course, where there is community, there is always the potential for commerce. Those enterprises which meet the fundamental needs of their community members for communication and for commerce will be the most successful.

## *WHAT DRAWS PEOPLE TO THE WEB AS A COMMUNITY?*

Consumers and businesses both have a need for certain types of community based on their particular needs. Among those needs are:

◆ *Transactions.* Communities organized around transactions bring people together who wish to buy and sell something, either products or services or information. For example, Wine.com sells wine, and eBay attracts millions of people come together to buy and sell collectibles and just about anything. Neither of these dot coms is a manufacturer or a vendor. They merely provide the platform to facilitate the buy-and-sell transaction. They have high business value and low interpersonal communication. An exception might be Amazon.com, which not only has high business value but a reasonably good degree of communication with its repeat customers. Regular visitors are welcomed with additional recommendations in their areas of interest as well as emails about new titles when they request such notification. Commercial applications of transaction-based communities, or B2B exchanges as they are known, are growing much faster than the B2C or consumer exchanges right now. Recent examples of major efforts in this area include: E-GM (the B2C connection with its dealers and customers) which recently joined Covisint in a B2B effort to capitalize on shared supply-chain advantages with its major competitors Ford, DaimlerChrysler; and General Electric which formed a huge exchange powered by Commerce One's platform in order to facilitate transactions with its more than 100,000 suppliers.

◆ *Affinity.* Here people come together because of similar interests. For example Garden.com, with a free signup, enables members to share information about any gardening topics, from plants to landscaping design tips, email the garden doctor on problems, 24-hour chat on certain topics, and purchase garden products from outside vendors. Another example of affinity is Salon.com. According to company filings, Salon.com is an Internet media company, headquartered in San Francisco, which produces a network of ten subject-specific, demographically targeted Web sites and a variety of online communities designed to attract premium Internet advertisers and electronic commerce partners. Business versions include HR.com (for human resources professionals). A good hybrid example is Martha StuartLiving.com which has a lot of useful information on things that people care about around the house, such as home improvement, crafts, cooking and decorating. It is also developing into a commerce portal. There are even communities for Windows 2000 users.

◆ *Support/relationship networks.* These involve people coming together around sharing certain common experiences in an online community. For example, at WebMD or DrKoop.com, registered members can get medical information, engage in chats, post to message boards, or find support for their community health efforts through the site. High interaction and personalization but low interaction among members. Other communities developing in this area cater for gender-specific audiences. For instance women have iVillage.com. And now those in mid-life and beyond have Third Age.com, a community portal catering to the needs of the booming gray-haired population.

◆ *Entertainment.* Fantasy, sports, and gaming. ESPN (now a part of Go.com) offers members the latest news about major sports and the ability to play or even create fantasy teams that compete with other members' teams over the Net. Other major networks with sites on the Web are FoxSports and CBSSportsline. Generally these sites have high interaction among members but very little commerce application. Sites like Yahoo!, Excite and Netscape are now offering a fair amount of sports news, both national and local but not to the degree that most sports afficionados require. Yahoo! even offers users the opportunity to assemble their own fantasy pro sports teams. Others offer more targeted sites such as GaySportsCentral, which will take users to gay, and lesbian sites devoted to particular sport activities. For pure entertainment information there are sites such as NYTheatre.com, a non-profit site covering just the New York City/Broadway theatre scene, and Theatre-link.com, which covers all aspects of the theatre on the Internet. Yahoo! has many links to its own and partner affiliate entertainment sites from its home site.

# BUILD OR BUY

In typical light-speed fashion, the community movement has gone from building to consolidation in the space of less than two years. And for portal builders with currency, like Yahoo!, it worked out just fine.

Community strategy requires continual expansion. Yahoo! was already experienced in its organized community building effort since it started Clubs in the summer of 1998. By January 1999 the company acquired GeoCities, a public company claiming to host more than 3.5 million Web sites.

According to Amy Sacharow, a new media analyst for Jupiter Communications (now part of Media Metrix), the consolidation was predictable because companies that depend on one form of technology or service like site creation or chat, "do not have stand-alone business models." Those "only offering community tools will either be acquired or consolidated." (Newsbytes News Network, Update January 28, 1999.) Media Metrix declared Yahoo!/GeoCities would attract more than 82 percent of the overall Web surfing public with their combined reach.

Less than a year later, Yahoo! further consolidated its community mindshare by purchasing eGroups, which was about to go public on its own. It merged eGroups' 17 million members and 800,000 active email groups with the Yahoo! community of 145 million members. In addition to the large member numbers, Yahoo! added many new personal and professional community groups to its growing family of members. According to Jeff Mallet in a company statement about the merger, the "addition of eGroups technology ... strengthens the communications services Yahoo!

currently provides users and gives them more ways to stay in touch with other individuals."

## GUIDING IDEAS FOR COMMUNITY BUILDERS

The consensus is that communities and community building will be around for at least the next several years as the first- and second-tier players battle for turf, and one or more sharp newcomers try to elbow their way into the market.

◆ *Provide the technology to empower the user*. The user will generate their personalized content. Once you establish a framework, remember that:

◆ *You no longer control the community*. The producer eventually becomes controlled by the users themselves. Yahoo!'s GeoCities acquisition allowed member-users to build their own communities. Once a community begins to flourish:

◆ *Support the community*. Provide ways for users to come together, communicate, pursue their interests, and conduct commerce.

Yahoo! has successfully built the quintessential online media model for both the consumer and business community. While it doesn't own its content like AOL and MSN, it is clearly a first-tier player. An interesting new player that has taken the lessons of the community model and applied it well is MarthaStewart.com. According to e-commerce experts Stacey Bressler and Charles Grantham in their book *Communities of Commerce* (McGraw-Hill, 2000), which is the first to take a detailed look at this revolutionary form of business, "the best example of this model of the future is the emergence of MarthaStewart.com. Stewart started out on a very small scale" and targeted a very narrow niche – the baby boomers. She was smart enough to understand this affluent niche market. "They are maturing and becoming interested in constructing around them a pleasant, comfortable place to live, raise their children, and entertain members of their community. Her first foray into this market was through limited television appearances, which expanded exponentially overnight. Her brand was established. More recently, she entered the publishing arena and established a community of commerce on the Internet." The next phase was to brand herself and take herself public, which she did in 1999 with a lot of support and money from some big names in the venture-capital community. (Stewart was once a financial consultant.) The smart money bet on the media model "as the successful model for the next decade. Martha Stewart has managed to develop a community of commerce, integrate it with television, print media, and the Internet, and attract investment from some of the most forward-thinking people in the business world." Bressler and Grantham think "the future is bright for those who understand" online business communities and "adopt a community-based way of doing business." And a final word of warning: "the future is bleak for those who don't."

> "... the future is bright for those who understand" online business communities and "adopt a community-based way of doing business."
> **– Stacey Bressler and Charles Grantham**

# REFERENCES

"Yahoo! Joins the Community Crowd," Newsbytes News Network, August 18, 1998.

Sugawara, Sandra (1999) Washington Post Foreign Service in the *Washington Post*, May 9, 1999.

Sigismund, Charles G. (2000) *Champions of Silicon Valley*, John Wiley & Sons, New York.

Michael White/Associated Press, the *Dallas Morning News*, November 22, 1999.

"Internet Competition," *Minneapolis Star Tribune*, May 30, 1999.

Newsbytes News Network, Update: "Yahoo! Confirms GeoCities Acquisitions," January 28, 1999.

Rheingold, Howard (1999) *The Virtual Community*, HarperCollins, New York.

# BILBLIOGRAPHY

Miller, Leslie (1998) "Homesteading the Net," *USA Today*, March 11, 1998.

Four

# GIVE USERS PLENTY OF REASONS FOR REPEAT VISITS

Y ahoo! started off as a directory of sites on the Internet. As a directory and a search engine, it could be reached directly or through other sites or search engines. It quickly revised its strategy to change from a search engine and directory of sites on the Internet to a portal in 1998, as the company realized it needed to evolve along with the rest of the Web. A fact of life on the Web is that maintaining eyeballs requires consistent if not continual reinvention.

Portals differ from search engines in depth and in scope. Portals are synonymous with gateways as they are take-off points for surfers on the Web. While they may begin as ISPs (Internet Service Providers), such as AOL or CompuServe, portals typically offer connectivity as well as a cluster of value-added services to users, from simple site directories, news, weather, free email, instant messaging, stock quotes, customization or personalization, electronic newsletters, community forums, chat rooms and e-commerce capabilities. While these are typically more than the average user will take advantage of, it is only a matter of time before portals will become a dominant feature in Web user activities. Gartner Group defines three strategies for portal development – win/place/show. The win strategy has familiar names in its space like Yahoo! AOL, Infoseek and Lycos to name a few. They dominate the pack with strong brand identity, interactive services, and aggregated content and ISP functionality. The goal here is to become a "network" for users (*Internet Week*, February 22, 1999). There are several reasons for this.

## PORTAL WARS: PHASE TWO

The amount of information on the Web is doubling every 100 days. Without an intelligent starting point, navigation – or at least searching the Web – will become so complex and top-heavy that portals will probably get the most visitors. Current examples of portals, aside from Yahoo!, are MSN, Infoseek – that with Disney has created the Go Network – and AltaVista to name a few. The next phase in portal development is already well under way. It's the specialty portal devoted to target areas of interest such as business, finance, games and so forth. A prime example of such a portal is Bullseye, which has a general search engine, a search engine by category, and a professional level, fee-based search engine with no banner advertising. Other specialty or vertical portals, also known as vortals, are developing along special interests or needs such as gardening (Garden.com), health (WebMD, DrKoop.com, OnHealth.com), jobsearch (Monster.com), directions (Mapquest.com) weather (Weather.com), and many others. Yahoo!'s strategy is to be the one place for everything, so it contains links to appropriate special interest sites but aggregates them all under the Yahoo! umbrella. It uses its name recognition to bring high traffic and add-ons to increase the time spent on the site.

> "... the keys to all aspects of Internet business are customization, personalization and relationship-building."
> – Peter Keen

## POWER SHIFTS TO THE USERS

Power on the Web is shifting from the information provider to the user. Eventually, consumers will be able to customize their own

# TWO PHASES OF E-COMMERCE DEVELOPMENT

Peter Keen talks about the two phases he calls chapters of e-commerce in his book *Electronic Commerce Relationships* (Prentice-Hall, 1999). In the first phase, it quickly became apparent that "the keys to all aspects of Internet business are customization, personalization and relationship-building." Portal players, such as Yahoo! and others, began to give away freebies to help build the relationship: email, Internet access, research, news articles and even PCs. Building repeat business and relationships set the stage for phase two: the move to maximum personalization. From the early use of "cookies" – files on your hard drive that identify you to an Internet site as a user – the push has been to give users a way to customize their preferred Web sites. Personalization became the basis of the portal player strategy. You build a relationship and a brand so customers park at your site to explore the Web, the way shoppers park at an anchor store, shop the rest of the mall, and return to the anchor store when they are leaving.

browsers and just pull up sharply targeted information they want to see on a regular basis. So in the future, the only thing that will keep users coming to a portal site is loyalty and customer satisfaction that result in repeat business. Consequently, a great deal of thinking and planning have gone into Web development that promotes good user experience.

## LET'S GET PERSONAL

An old-economy business tenet that survives even today is to know your customer. Thanks to technology it's now possible to accumulate the necessary information to know your customer better than ever. The way that portals and e-commerce sites get to know their customers is by following their trail. By use of clickstream data – the trail you leave behind as you move through a site – the company can determine your individual behaviors and habits on a site and then tailor content accordingly. Down the road, the potential is that each user will experience different content on the same site.

## YAHOO! ANY WAY YOU WANT IT!

The Internet has grown so quickly and so broadly that the only way search engines can even attempt to cover it is by going a mile wide and skin deep. Even that's an understatement according to a young private company out of Sioux Falls, South Dakota. Bright Planet has developed brand new software to plumb the depths of the Internet, revealing what it terms the "deep Web" or the invisible material out there that we never see (or perhaps may not want to). While this "invisible Internet" universe is no doubt of keen interest to professional researchers and a mysterious attraction for those serious explorers who spend their days and nights searching the Internet's inner space, for most of us the specialized search engine is what's needed to give the exponentially growing mass of content available a more meaningful context.

> The way that portals and e-commerce sites get to know their customers is by following their trail.

Yahoo!'s mission has been to offer its users a way to dynamically organize and otherwise integrate a ton of content from various

Yahoo! properties according to their personal preferences, so they may customize their browsing experience.

# ATTRACT NEW, AND RETAIN REPEAT USERS

Early in the game, Yahoo! was aware of, and focused on, the need to not only attract, but also retain new users without ignoring its existing and frequent user base. User data was collected and analyzed and used in careful calculations to determine that the key to this type of retention was contained in providing individuals with the ability to customize the portal to their own specific needs and interests. Tim Koogle addressed the success of this strategy of data crunching saying, "The result is a powerful self-reinforcing distribution platform for an ever-increasing array of content, communications services and merchant services. It also drives a great business model when managed."

In addition to Yahoo!'s obvious success, recent statistics support this early decision, reporting that people who personalize their own site return five times more often than people who don't. (Joe Kraus, senior vice-president and co-founder of *Excite*, as quoted to Mathew McAllister author of LIFE IN CYBERSPACE/Portals: Gateways To the Net, and Ads, *Newsday* June 10, 1998.)

# ALCHEMY: SECRETS OF THE PORTAL-DEVELOPER'S ART

The key to getting frequent repeat users back to a portal is to give them some control over their displays and features just like the options available on a car and more recently in some electronic equipment. But just what features and displays to give them control over is a part of the portal developer's art. Attracting repeat users to a portal requires an understanding of the habits of frequent users and what motivates them to get on line. Fortunately the user-tracking data on Web sites can be thoroughly analyzed to provide clues to what users prefer the most. By looking at that data, Yahoo! was able to determine that they needed a twofold approach.

Users who go online to meet other people prefer community platforms and applications like discussion forums or chat rooms, as we discussed in Chapter 3. The second audience, the ones who principally seek information, look for content and accessibility features. This requires the creation of services that are used daily, such as local weather information or personally chosen stock quotes. This creates an incentive for people to invest in customization of the site and will bring people back to the site frequently enough to bookmark it. (Jennifer Bailey, Netscape Web-site division vice-president, Netscape.)

# THE EVOLUTION OF MY YAHOO!

"Now, more than ever before," Ralph Averbuch, Yahoo!'s senior producer was quoted as saying, "the ability to select the information you want from the wealth of content on the Web is vital. As the Internet becomes part of people's day-to-day lives, they want easy access to the information they're most interested in." Yahoo! met this need through the introduction to the market of My Yahoo! Says Averbuch, "My Yahoo! is a simple and effective way to bring relevant content directly to the individual." (Author unknown, "YAHOO!: Go on – get personal ... with my Yahoo!

Make the web your web with a personalized information page,"
*M2 PressWIRE*, January 10, 1999.)

So just what can be customized in My Yahoo!?

To start with, Yahoo! is vast. It's grown into a sizable collection
of media properties that are expanding on their own just like
our ever-expanding galaxy, the Milky Way. Among the different
types of content that can be customized or personalized on the
My Yahoo! page, developers made sure they provided Yahoo!
users with many richly-featured tools. As a result, they have all
the means necessary to tailor their screen page to suit personal
tastes and information requirements. Specifically:

◆ *Searching.* At the center of Yahoo!'s universe – and front
and center on the My Yahoo! page – is the familiar search
button.

◆ *News headlines.* Whether it's national and international news
via Reuters or Yahoo!'s other partners like the Associated
Press or ABC News, you can get national and international
highlights and full text stories organized around your speci-
fied areas of interest.

◆ *Finance.* Yahoo! Finance is familiar to many users. It has
developed a regular following among stock jockeys like us and
it happens to be one of the leading personal-finance sites on
the Web. Any portfolios or personalized stock quotes you've
set up are automatically fed to your My Yahoo! page. Note:
there are so many additional customizable options for My
Yahoo! that avid users are advised to check these out in one
of the new books that have been published, such as *Yahoo!
For Dummies*, by Brad Hill, (IDG Books, 2000). There are

simply too many amazing facets of Yahoo! to cover here. We are just giving you the Cliff Notes from *Hamlet*. Hill has done an excellent job of delving into them for those who want to get the most out of Yahoo! without digging on their own.

◆ *Neighborhood entertainment*. Entering your zip code gets you everything from showtimes for flicks at local theaters to TV listings.

◆ *Message center*. The Yahoo! Messenger feature alerts you when new emails hit your box, as well as a calendar for business and personal items. The Yahoo! Calendar is a simple way to stay organized.

◆ *Sports*. From local team action to sports headlines that match your preferences, you can even get up-to-the-minute scores on games in progress whenever you refresh the page.

◆ *Weather*. From local forecasts, you can extend your reach to capture climatic conditions at your favorite vacation spot or second home.

◆ *Other daily features*. These are expanding all the time. Recent additions include "Yahoo! Points for frequent shopping, medical questions and answers, and health and entertainment features.

## More personalization features

The My Yahoo! page has left- and right-side features and departments. On the left side there are selections for records, bill paying, bookmarks, chat rooms, maps, and package tracking, to name a few. Right-side personalization options include your address book, clubs, fitness, horoscopes (if you list your birthday), message boards you subscribe to, phone searching, small business tips, Yellow Pages, and much more.

My Yahoo! provides direct access to various services such as free email, instant stock quotes, chat rooms, news headlines, search engines, access to various Internet service providers, free software, air tickets, books and many other products and services. In other words, most of what an average net user wants from the whole Internet. As well as the local content, the user can adapt guides around the world, and pages at any time, to add new information as desired.

We should mention some of the things or properties that aren't available on My Yahoo!, at least not as we went to press. They are: Yahooligans and Yahoo! Internet Life. The teens and kids site is still for kids' eyes only. Yahoo! Computers, a very practical property has to be explored separately, although there are Computer Tips on My Yahoo! that are condensed from there. And Yahoo! Finance is such a robust property that what you can get on My Yahoo! barely scratches the surface. In short, to appreciate the richness and depth of these services you'll have to go there.

## Keeping registration set-up simple

My Yahoo! has been careful to keep the initial time required to register its new users to a minimum. Once signed on, users are asked to provide a username, password, and email address as well as demographic information which is forwarded to advertisers to assist targeting their advertisements, messages and updates to specific audiences. Those who register, are also asked to select topics of interest which are used to set up news feeds within related areas of interest. The option to select specific stocks for monitoring is also made available.


## YAHOO! FOR ALL YOUR DAILY NEEDS

Users are encouraged to set up the Web page with information that they have selected as pertinent. Upon bringing up the page, the user is automatically greeted with selections from the day's top news in specific categories such as technology and entertainment. The previously described 14 categories are also included with direct links from which users gain quick access from their homepage which acts as the hub in a hub-and-spoke construction. Nothing is overlooked, as even the ability to categorize direct links to chat rooms, clubs, and even personal ads is included under the category Connect – everything to hook the occasional relationship-oriented user who casually stops by.

The integral, top-left-side Message Center contains daily essentials for personal use, including an address book and daily calendar complete with automatic reminders once loaded with the user's important dates. The storage of such obviously personal information by millions demonstrates not only the complete willingness of My Yahoo! users to become dependent on Yahoo! on a daily basis, but the extent to which My Yahoo! was designed to address every aspect of an Internet user's daily experience.

Users are never locked in to any decisions, and with a simple keystroke they can modify any aspect of their My Yahoo! page instantaneously.

## Adding depth to user features

With the $81 million purchase of Four11 Corporation, users were provided with the option of email accounts with direct access and links to My Yahoo! (*Fortune*, March 2, 1998). To further address users' total communications needs, other features such as instant messaging were also included, which further boosted My Yahoo!'s daily usefulness.

This daily use also came as a result of My Yahoo!'s willingness to cooperate rather than compete with the different media available to the public. To that extent, My Yahoo! provided its users with options including local daily television listings, local movie listings, sports scores and game listings and even the text of daily newspapers.

# YAHOO! FIRST AND FOREMOST

To ensure that users were not tempted away by the competition, My Yahoo!, could be set up as each users' default homepage so it would lead the user there directly and would be the first page seen each time the user went online. This proved an enticing proposition for users, and when coupled with free Internet access through partnerships with Spiegel.com and Bluelight.com, My Yahoo! began to rival the images of AOL and Microsoft Network. Over 30 million people shop at Kmart weekly. Many of them will also check in at Bluelight. Most important of all, My Yahoo! remains true to Jerry Yang's and David Filo's original vision of keeping Yahoo! free for the end-user; "We are committed to keeping Yahoo! free for the

end-user while continuing to add enhancements," Mr Yang
was quoted as saying (*USA Today*, April 13, 1995).

## ADDING THE NEIGHBORHOOD TOUCH

Once the attention of the user was guaranteed, filing all the
available categories for selection had to be addressed. Yahoo!
began its focus by enhancing its own proprietary site offerings
on My Yahoo! Their focus on sites such as Yahoo! Auctions
enabled these sites to grow to unprecedented sizes. "Yahoo!
Auctions offers a uniquely comprehensive, global and integrated commerce platform for sellers to
distribute their products in multiple for-
mats to the world's largest consumer
audience," said Tony Surtees,
Yahoo!'s vice-president and general manager of commerce. Yahoo!
used its proprietary site offerings
to further expand its international
presence by introducing local auction
services to more than 14 countries, including Brazil, Denmark and Korea. Through the use of
Yahoo! Auctions, sellers and buyers can market items around
the globe in 11 languages. An example of the success of these
proprietary sites is evident in Yahoo! Japan Auctions, which
launched on September 29, 1999. It has grown to be one of
the leading person-to-person auction sites in Japan with more
than 30,000 simultaneous daily auctions reinforcing Yahoo!'s
position as the most extensive network of globally-branded,
localized online auctions services in the world.

> "We are committed to keeping Yahoo! free for the end-user while continuing to add enhancements."
> – Jerry Yang

"From shopping and distributing merchandise through Yahoo! Auctions, we enable users to build their businesses on the Web. Our commerce solutions work together to allow retailers of all sizes to test new products, new releases, new markets and find the right pricing levels. Yahoo! is the place people know they can come to find, compare, buy or sell almost anything they want, the way they want, whenever and wherever they want," said Tony Surtees.

Yahoo! went beyond growing their own proprietary sites, by partnering with online content providers to ensure user access to a majority of available Web sites. Links to each Web site could be incorporated into a My Yahoo! page in a mutual win-win situation, whereby My Yahoo! provided the user with the convenience of creating personalized one-stop shopping, while virtually guaranteeing repeat business from new users. In addition, My Yahoo! partnerships helped establish the Internet industry's culture of building relationships and striking deals. Any company that owns a portal site inevitably needs to create business arrangements with many of the companies to which the portal links. Koogle addressed these partnerships reporting, "We, of course, do lots and lots of partnerships, hundreds of them around the globe now, probably 600 or 700 content providers who are at this point under contract ... great partners of ours." (Fox News Network, December 1, 1999)

> Yahoo! went beyond growing their own proprietary sites by partnering with online content providers to ensure user access to a majority of available Web sites.

# GIVING KIDS CONTEXT FOR CONTENT, FOR KIDS ONLY – YAHOOLIGANS

Rather than simply focusing on the content available through the initial My Yahoo! portal, Yahoo! also began to create portals within the main portal which were specifically aimed at other subsets such as children. "There are currently no Web homes for kids that provide them with a context for surfing on the Internet," said Jeff Mallet, senior vice-president of business operations at Yahoo! "However, kids comprise one of the fastest-growing groups on the Internet and Yahoo!" In response, Yahoo! created Yahooligans, a site self-described as "a site that 'completely surrounds the young Web user.'" While the Yahooligans interface retains the familiar look and feel of the regular Yahoo! site, it "integrates youth-oriented content and graphics and is the first site dedicated to engaging them in compelling Internet discovery."

To enhance its own knowledge, which had up to that point focused almost exclusively on adults, Yahoo! partnered with Ingenius, a company that specializes in online entertainment and educational products for kids, to handle the selection of linked sites and develop a rating system to weed out potentially harmful content from the directory. In addition, Yahoo! partnered with SurfWatch Software to promote child-safety issues in a Street Smart Safety section of Yahooligans. The Street Smart Safety section offered Internet safety tips for children and parents, with a low-cost version of SurfWatch to parents of Yahooligans users, which would allow unwanted sexually explicit material on the Internet to be blocked (Newsbytes News Network, March 19, 1996). But more importantly, Yahoo! was defining and addressing the needs of future generations of Internet users commonly referred to as the I-Generation. By shaping this generation's use of the Internet, Yahooligans was ensuring that Yahoo! would be in the position later to continue to best serve their needs.

## ZIP OVER TO GET LOCAL

Another subportal – also customizable – is Get Local, available from the front page of Yahoo! as well as from links in Yahoo!'s regional hierarchy. Get Local is customized through the use of a city or zip code. Users then have access to information on that location, including yellow pages, driving directions, weather forecasts, scores for area teams, UPI news headlines, free classifieds, message boards, city maps, TV listings, local movie locations and showing times and white pages. In addition, the information is updated regularly. Ironically, this portal also acts as a city guide, as users can change the corresponding information from city to city with a simple stroke of the "Change City" icon in the lower right corner of the page.

> Yahoo! Finance offers its users a simplified option to manage and aggregate all aspects of their finances in one location and with the use of only one secure login.

## THE 800-POUND GORILLA PROPERTY – YAHOO! FINANCE

The final customizable subportal set which merits particular attention, is Yahoo!'s effort to empower people with its suite of online financial tools through the introduction of Yahoo! Finance.

Everyday, millions of users sign on to Yahoo! Finance even if they don't necessarily visit the other Yahoo! properties. This portal is rich with information about listed companies, stock, bonds and options, as well as domestic and world market activity. However, this is merely the surface level of the toolset available on the site.

Yahoo! Finance offers its users a simplified option to manage and aggregate all aspects of their finances in one location and with the use of only one secure login. Partnering with such companies as E*Trade and Telebank, Yahoo! links with a number of outside services, such as brokerage and bank accounts respectively, which users may already be utilizing in addition to Yahoo!'s proprietary offerings.

Clients with E*Trade brokerage accounts, for example, enjoy the features and benefits of a Yahoo! Finance portfolio, which includes such features as customizing portfolio-specific quotes and news to integration with other Yahoo! properties, like My Yahoo! and Yahoo! Calendar. In addition, as E*Trade customers enter trading orders with E*Trade during the day, they can also access their updated portfolio holdings on Yahoo! Finance. Yahoo!

"Providing our registered users with access to their personal brokerage account information gives them the ability to enjoy the convenience and flexibility associated with managing their finances online at one, centralized location," said Tim Brady, senior vice-president of network services. "These (agreements) support our commitment to provide users with personalized information from a wide array of leading Internet companies." (*Business Wire*, May 23, 2000) It all amounts to an impressive collection of highly valuable financial information on a particularly sought-after demographic.

# PARTNERING TO BRING THE BEST OF THE BEST TO YAHOO! FINANCE

Never allowing themselves to rest, Yahoo! Finance continues to push forward by creating relationships that give its users increased access to financial information. The partnership with Telebank was the first to provide users with direct access to their bank accounts through a portal. "By adding Telebank to our existing online account access service on Yahoo! Finance we are continuing to expand the value-added services we offer our millions of users," said Mr Brady. "We are very pleased to be working with Telebank, as our relationship with them provides our users with more choice and flexibility when it comes to managing their personal finances online." (*Business Wire*, July 28, 1999)

Yahoo! partnered with outside companies to provide its own proprietary offerings. Yahoo! Bill Pay, also available on Yahoo! Finance, provides a service which enables Yahoo!'s users in the United States to securely pay bills online. Realizing the need to differentiate its own proprietary services from the competition, Yahoo! partnered with CheckFree Corporation, an established provider of financial electronic commerce, that allows its users to electronically pay bills not only to established companies, but also to individuals including landlords, family members and friends. In addition the partnership provided the service with the ability to make payments of differing amounts every month, schedule fixed monthly payments, such as car or mortgage payments or schedule single payments, such as car registration or tuition fees, up to one year in advance.

"Yahoo! consistently brings our users the best of the Web, and providing them with the ability to pay bills online is an extension of this commitment. Making sure users have their varying personal financial needs met by Yahoo! Finance is one of the keys to its incredible success," said Mr Brady. (*Business Wire*, September 8, 1999)

Yahoo!'s latest move to boost the stickiness of their prime community property centers around one of the biggest new growth areas in consumer commerce, the online management of financial accounts or financial aggregation of account information in one location.

> "Bringing users' personal financial account information to one location, online account aggregation provides users with a unique perspective of their financial situation, giving users increased control when it comes to managing their finances," said Tim Sheehan, director of production, Yahoo! Finance. "As a trusted and objective source of information, our users asked Yahoo! for a convenient way to manage all of their personalized content and activities at one secure location and with one user ID and password. Yahoo!'s relationship with VerticalOne allows consumers to do this, and we are very pleased to be working with VerticalOne in this endeavor."

> Today's announcement is an expansion of Yahoo!'s existing online access program, which currently allows registered Yahoo! users to view their account information from a variety of financial institutions, including Bank of America, Deutsche Bank, National Westminster Bank, E*TRADE, and TD Waterhouse. Yahoo! Finance, one of the most popular financial sites on the Internet, provides users with a broad range of comprehensive financial services and information. As a leading financial destination, Yahoo! Finance is rapidly becoming the place Web users go to in order to perform important tasks related to

their finances and view all of their personal financial account information in one convenient place. My Yahoo! gives each user his or her own customized view of the Web, and with today's launch of this service, users can now access the most personalized data available yet on My Yahoo! (Company Web-site Press Release, August 30, 2000).

The success of providing these available services for selection, as well as the subportals such as Yahooligans and Yahoo! Finance has grown to the point where Yahoo! Inc. and Sequoia Software Corporation recently partnered to offer software to corporate information technology managers to add personalization features to their own portals (*e-Week*, July 3, 2000). This partnership utilizes the services of integration-software developer TIBCO to extend the personalization features of My Yahoo! to e-business companies. This innovation would enable businesses to create tailored corporate portals on top of the company's own Web portal infrastructure. The lure is to offer companies the ability to combine the functionality and content of My Yahoo! with company-defined information (*Windows*, January 1, 1999, p. 50).

My Yahoo!'s presence on the Internet extends its early-mover leads through the sheer volume of both its proprietary and partnership-based offerings. Providing access to both the entirety and enormity of the entire Internet community, from international auctions to more narrowly relevant information such as the time schedule of the local movie house, has certainly increased user interest in My Yahoo! However as quickly as the bulk of this available information may attract user interest, the need to wade through this mountain of information is guaranteed to quickly scare these same users away. My Yahoo!'s success lies in providing the user with the ability to select only that information which is relevant to him or her and creating a personalized path from which to cruise the Internet.

Once again, as we have pointed out before, the thinking behind the architecture of the advanced properties was based on human factors. Colin Furness, a senior information architect at Iguana Studios, a Web-design company in New York that has designed sites for the Zagat restaurant guides, among others, points out that the job of the information architect has become increasingly important in today's Web world. It's the one place (the Web) where the rule "if you build it, they will come" simply doesn't apply. The technology has to be adapted to suit the needs of the people, not the other way around. "The world has been slow to realize that the Web is nothing more than a very big information system that can benefit from the same attention to human factors" as, say, your new house (*New York Times*, August 7, 2000). This simple philosophy appears not to be lost on the architects and developers at Yahoo!

## BUILDING THE "HIGH FREQUENCY" CUSTOMER RELATIONSHIP

◆ *Know your customer.* With the use of software tracking or clickstream analysis, you can learn just what users go to, how often they go there and how they find their way there. Also make use of electronic feedback and listen to what your customers tell you they want.

◆ *Strive to improve functionality.* Yahoo! does an outstanding job of providing information and improving the utility of its site based on what their registered users say they want. The power is shifting to users and those who listen well to them and provide aggregated services across a broad spectrum of needs will win their loyalty. When Yahoo! added its free email for life it quickly aggregated so many users that it now has the largest number of email accounts. Given that email still constitutes the largest use of the Internet, the company has successfully laid another durable frequency plank in their ubiquitous platform.

◆ *Expand pages.* Perhaps Miss Piggy was right: more is more. In the land of the Web, there seems to be no end in sight to the expansion possibilities. But the secret is in adding pages without sacrificing ease of use for the consumer. So far, Yahoo! seems to have the best of both worlds.

◆ *Add convenience features.* More and more the Web is about convenience. There's no denying that there is a bond growing between people and their computers. Like the telephone, it's becoming a part of our daily lives. Sites offering convenience and new services that help the consumer or user to manage or organize their lives better will come out winners. Examples: financial account aggregation, which Yahoo! Finance added, makes it possible for consumers to access their credit-card, brokerage and bank-account balances in one place. Big winner, Yahoo! Big losers, the financial institutions like banks and brokerages, who will jealously guard privacy of information from one another. The big plus is that Yahoo! will be able to develop new services around the information the aggregation brings, without sacrificing privacy. Other ideas: Web-based address books and calendars, and Web-based bookmarks so you can access your favorite sites from any computer.

# REFERENCES

Smith, David (1999) *Internet Week*, February 22, 1999.

Keen, P., Ballance, C., Chan, S., and Schrump, S. (1999) *Electronic Commerce Relationships: Trust by Design*, (ed. Peter Keen) Prentice-Hall, New York.

Stross, Randall E. (1998) "How Yahoo! Won The Search Wars," *Fortune*, March 2, 1998.

Miller, Leslie "Yahoo: The Homespun Web Map" *USA Today*, April 13, 1995.

Cavuto, Neil (1999) "Yahoo! – Chairman and CEO," *The Cavuto Business Report*, Fox News Network, December 1, 1999.

Bowers, Richard (1996) "More On Yahoo!'s Yahooligans For Kids," Newsbytes News Network, March 19, 1996.

"Yahoo! and Telebank Launch Online Account Integration; Yahoo! Enhances Online Account Access Service with Addition of Telebank," *Business Wire*, July 28, 1999.

"Yahoo! Announces Availability of Bill Payment Services; Yahoo! Teams with CheckFree to Provide Millions of Users with Ability to Pay Bills Online," *Business Wire*, September 8, 1999.

"Yahoo! Gives Consumers Online Access to Brokerage Account Information," *Business Wire*, May 23, 2000.

Press Release, August 30, 2000.

DuBois, Grant (2000) "Portals Getting Personal," *e-Week*, July 3, 2000.

Ulanoff, Lance (1999) "Windows News: Portals Target Business Users," *Windows*, January 1, 1999, p. 50.

Bierdorfer, J.D. (2000) "Information Architect makes the Web Work," *New York Times*, August 7, 2000.

Five

# PARTNER WITH THE BEST

# THE ART OF THE PARTNERSHIP

A well-developed talent to create and maintain profitable partnerships gives companies a significant leg-up on their competition in today's global marketplace. Experts often call this "collaborative advantage" – a connection between two independent organizations that provides immediate value for both sides while keeping the door open for any new opportunities that may arise in the future.

Yahoo! has turned partnerships into a strategic art form by creating hundreds of relationships with companies worldwide during the past few years. "Since the founding of Yahoo!, we have been aggressive in partnering globally with leading suppliers of technology, content, merchant services and communication services," Koogle noted in the company's 1998 Annual Report. "Developing this expertise has been a key internal goal and one which should serve us well in aggressively growing our business in the future of this highly competitive industry."

In this chapter, we'll look at the ingredients that make for successful partnerships and how Yahoo! applied these principles in many key business relationships that have fueled its success in the business-to-consumer marketplace. And we'll also look at how Yahoo! will use this partnership strategy to support its more recent entry into the fiercely competitive business-to-business arena.

## Anatomy of a successful partnership

Successful partnerships are more than just deal-making. These relationships work only when both partners can bring something of value to the table. More specifically, each partner must provide complementary assets and skills that are essential to create win-win results for everyone involved.

> The reasoning for entering into a partnership is rather simple. Partners must *need* each other.

The reasoning for entering into a partnership is rather simple. Partners must *need* each other. Given the speed and cost of technological change, as well as increased expenses for personnel and administration, companies quickly realize that they can't go it alone. Future success depends on the ability to share costs, skills, information, technology, access to markets – and even capital – with others.

The resulting relationship, however, has to fit comfortably into the major strategic objectives of both partners, and support each other's long-term goals. Objectives need to be clearly stated. Each partner must understand operating procedures and their particular responsibilities. Performance assessments should be conducted regularly, supported by contingency plans on how to respond when such unexpected events as market-driven changes occur. Otherwise, such relationships will fail.

## Partnerships as strategic vision: give consumers a choice

Early on, Yahoo! understood the importance of partnering with businesses that could provide the assets and skills it needed to become more than just an Internet search engine. In an interview with *Time* magazine (November 1, 1997), Yang explained how the company had changed its perspective a year earlier. When looking to develop commerce capabilities in early 1996, Yahoo! was intent on developing its own centralized shopping mall and initiated one of its first partnerships with Visa to make it happen.

But Yang and company continued to keep one eye on the marketplace and quickly realized that certain segments, such as books, music and stock trades, were maturing much faster in terms of electronic commerce development. In the light of Yahoo!'s strategic mission of "putting the user first and delivering the best Web experience available," the company switched gears.

"Instead of building a mall that has everything, we decided it would be more effective and better for the user if we thread, embed and put shopping options in the context of the yahoo.com site," he added.

That initial change in mind-set continues to this day as Yahoo! seeks out strategic business partnerships in several areas, including technology, content, distribution, e-commerce and communication services. The company notes that it receives hundreds of proposals each month for review.

This focus on partnerships also continues to astound the many experts and analysts who remain skeptical that Yahoo!'s long-standing policy – what some call "content agnostic" – of connecting users to a wide variety of content on the Internet but owning very little of it will keep them competitive, particularly in light of recent industry consolidations.

# PARTNERSHIP BUILDING

Business relationships are a lot like marriages. Success often depends on the ability for both partners to change their mind-set from "I" to "we."

Management guru Rosabeth Moss Kanter has studied a wide variety of business partnerships and alliances over the years. From her research, she has identified eight criteria that companies must meet in order to achieve a similar mind-set, what she calls "The Eight I's That Create Successful We's" (*Harvard Business Review*, July 1, 1994, p. 96):

◆ *Individual excellence.* Each partner must be strong and able to contribute something of value to the partnership. Motives focus on pursuing future opportunities, not trying to compensate for inherent weaknesses.

◆ *Importance.* The relationship must be based on strategic objectives for both partners. The partnership plays a role in achieving long-term goals.

◆ *Interdependence.* Partners must need each other, and have complementary skills and assets that, when combined, can generate results which each partner could not obtain on their own.

◆ *Investment.* Partners need to invest in each other as a way to demonstrate their respective stakes in the relationship and long-term commitment.

◆ *Information.* Communication is open, *and* partners readily share information they need to make the relationship work.

◆ *Integration.* Partners build broad connections between many people at many organizational levels in an effort to work together smoothly.

◆ *Institutionalization.* The relationship maintains a formal status, with clear responsibilities and decision processes.

◆ *Integrity.* Partners interact in a way that shows mutual trust and
never try to undermine each other.

The heat was turned up particularly high on Yahoo! in early
2000 following announcement of the AOL Time Warner pow-
erhouse and the subsequent drop in Yahoo!'s stock price.
Analysts, experts and even amateur pundits were placing bets
that Yahoo! would now need to go out and find itself a media
institution to stay in the game. Arthur Newman, an analyst at
Schroder & Co, noted in a report that although the company
doubled revenues and traffic during fourth quarter 1999, its
desire to remain independent and not merge with another
major company "could hurt it over the long term as competitors increasingly control both brand and distribution channels."
(Reuters, January 12, 2000.)

Yahoo!'s response was to remain steadfast in its role as a third-
party content aggregator created through its partnerships.
"Our strategy has always been to just distribute the content,"
Mallet told Reuters, adding that, in his opinion, consumers
still value a choice of different brands more than they do a
singular brand. He noted, in particular, Disney's celebrated
acquisition of Infoseek in 1999. "That hasn't been a home run,
to say the least," Mallet added.

## W³ partnership power

As we noted earlier, the list of partnerships Yahoo! has created
since 1996 is extremely lengthy and could easily fill a book by
itself. Instead, we'll look at the role partnerships have played
throughout Yahoo!'s history and focus on those that have

generated some of the greatest successes in the company's
development.

Early on, Yahoo!'s focus was on building content and advertising to attract more users to its services. As Koogle noted in
the company's fourth quarter 1996 report: "We will continue
to place a higher priority on investing heavily in building the
Yahoo! service and extending the Yahoo! brand on a global
scale, than delivering short-term profits."

"The increase in Yahoo!'s popularity and acceptance during this
past year would not have been possible without the tremendous
support we have received from users, advertisers and partners,"
Yang noted in the same report.

Yahoo! in 1996 certainly had advertisers – numbering 550 at
year's end – who represented a diverse range of products and
services. American Express, American Airlines, Avon, Bank
of America, Charles Schwab, Coca-Cola, Compaq Computers,
Disney, Ford Motor Company, General Mills, General Motors,
Hilton, IMB, Intuit, Intel, Nabisco, Publishers Clearing House,
Sony, Toyota, Virgin Records, Visa and Wal-Mart were some
of the new or repeat advertisers attracted to Yahoo!'s targeted
interactive advertising capabilities.

That year, Yahoo! and Proctor & Gamble, the largest consumer
advertiser in the US, began a customized, multi-month promotional campaign to link Yahoo! users with several P&G
brands on the Internet. Yahoo! worked with P&G to develop a
customized traffic-building program, determine ad scheduling,
rotation and placement, and provide creative guidelines for
all promotional elements.

"The program with P&G shows advertisers and agencies that Yahoo! is committed to meeting individual advertiser needs," sales director Anil Singh said in a May 1996 company announcement. "Our goal is to continue to lead the industry with creative, tailored programs and develop solutions for advertisers that truly take advantage of this powerful new media."

From the content perspective, Yahoo! was entering in partnerships to broaden its depth and range of information. In June of that year, Yahoo! and Granite Broadcasting Corporation announced a ground-breaking television–Internet alliance. This partnership integrated relevant Web sites and information into the Granite newscasts as well as its stations' Web sites, while Yahoo! gained access to local news feeds from Granite.

> From the content perspective, Yahoo! was entering in partnerships to broaden its depth and range of information.

This partnership represented a major change in how television news was gathered and disseminated, and the president of Granite Broadcasting at that time, Stuart J. Beck, went so far as to say the partnership would improve television's reputation as more than just a superficial delivery system. "For the first time, television viewers will take charge of the news with easy access to detailed information on the news most important to them," he said in a company statement.

Yahoo!, on the other hand, touted the partnership as a way for the company to become a "voice of the World Wide Web" while supporting its ongoing strategy to tailor unique content for new media property development and serve the needs of local communities.

# EXTENDING THE SERVICE PLATFORM

By 1997, Yahoo! was on a big roll in terms of developing partnerships, particularly those that could expand network programming and services for both its regional and national Web properties. The company teamed up with AudioNet to offer users access to audio and video Internet broadcasts for events related to categories and shared interest areas. Initially launched through Yahoo! Sports and Yahoo! Net Events, the agreement also called for further integration in other relevant areas. A partnership with The Sporting News and SportsTicker also added more comprehensive information and original content.

In the commerce areas, Yahoo! partnered with Microsoft Car-Point to provide one-click access to information on buying, selling and researching new and used automobiles. The company also created a relationship with Sabre, a leader in electronic travel transactions, to be the exclusive co-branded provider of travel booking services for Yahoo! users through its Travelocity service on Yahoo! Travel. Partnerships with Reel.com and VideoServe.com also created one-button access for movie video purchases.

In a CNBC interview in 1998, Koogle talked about how such commerce partnerships developed during the past year had proved beneficial to the company's bottom line. "The premier commerce partnerships we had in the most recent quarter represented about 15 percent of revenues," he said (CNBC/Dow Jones Business Video, February 26, 1998).

"It's an interesting extension of the natural platform we've built in advertising," Koogle added, noting that such partnerships provided advertisers with more than just high-visibility placement on the site. "They're getting a little more high status, if you will, and definitely long-term status by doing this," he added.

# EXPANDING DISTRIBUTION TO DRIVE TRAFFIC

But one other aspect of partnerships exploded during 1997. These concerned distribution of Yahoo! services designed to generate more traffic to its Web properties and compete against its leading competitor, AOL.

A relationship with GeoCities (which would later become a Yahoo! acquisition – discussed in the next chapter) offered Yahoo! users a free customized personal home page service. The plan also included Yahoo! to become the premier navigational guide, as well as provider of free personalized member services, for the GeoCities audience.

In addition, the company entered into a partnership with MCI to develop a co-marketed online service called Yahoo! Online, launched in early 1998. Under this arrangement, each company offered a disk – much like the omnipresent AOL disk – that provided both Internet access (powered by MCI Internet) and content from Yahoo! Users paid $14.95 per month for the first three months of service, which increased to $19.95 unless users signed up for MCI's long-distance telephone services.

As Koogle told CNBC, these partnerships were key to developing a growing awareness among the public that Yahoo! was more than just a search engine. "We've been building that [awareness] all along, and it's been apparent to our users for quite a while now that we have been way broader than just having a search engine capability or just a directory." But such distribution partnerships, he added, would create an incremental user stream by introducing Yahoo! to those who were just getting connected online for the first time.

Those distribution partnerships continued well into 1998 on a global basis. Besides arrangements with Compaq, Gateway and Microsoft's MSN and Web TV, Yahoo! also entered into co-branding partnerships with IBM for its Aptiva PCs. It also launched Yahoo! Click with British Telecommunications (BT), a service that combined BT Internet access with integration of Yahoo! UK and Yahoo! Ireland.

## FEEDING THE MULTITUDES

In 1999, Yahoo! focused on two significant objectives: to continue serving its growing audience, which had doubled to more than 120 million unique users, through integrated communications, commerce and media, and to provide the most effective interactive marketing platform for advertisers and merchants. It was also during this year that Yahoo! experienced its most successful financial quarter in the company's history.

By the end of the year, more than 9000 merchants had joined its Yahoo! Shopping platform, including such retailers as Barnes & Noble, Brooks Brothers, Eddie Bauer, Gap, Toys "R" Us, Victoria's Secret and Zales. Its merchant and advertiser base blossomed as well, increasing by more than 3500 and included some 1200 companies from outside the US, including Daewoo, Nokia, Norwegian Cruise Lines and Telefonica.

Yahoo! also began partnering with key players to provide banking and online bill-paying services. Their relationship with Deutsche Bank 24 to provide online banking services to Yahoo! Germany users and Deutsche Bank 24 customers represented the first time a German bank and an Internet media company had joined forces to provide online account access. In addition, this partnership included the launch of a co-branded credit card in February 2000, offering customers 24-hour access to their balance and transaction histories, for checking credit-card and savings accounts.

Other globally focused banking-related partnerships also occurred that year, including Banque Directe in France, Banca 121 in Italy, and Kookmin Bank in Korea.

Meanwhile in the US, Yahoo! teamed up with CheckFree Corporation, a leading provider of financial electronic commerce since 1981, to create Yahoo! E-Bills, a service for registered users that allows them to receive, review and pay their bills online. In addition to making payments of differing amounts each month, E-Bills offers greater flexibility in that individuals can set up fixed monthly payments for car loans and mortgage payments, as well as schedule up to a year-in-advance single payments, such as vehicle registration and tuition fees.

As Yahoo! entered the 21st century, its strategy for growing partnerships did not waver. In the content and marketing arenas, it developed new relationships with companies such as Healtheon to provide online research and access to a wide variety of healthcare information, and expanded an ongoing relationship with AutoWeb.com to provide users with direct access to the site's comprehensive buying service for new and pre-owned automobiles.

Distribution efforts continued to grow as Yahoo! enhanced its partnership with Hewlett Packard to offer access to My Yahoo! and Yahoo! Small Business for owners of new HP OmniBook XE Notebook and HP Brio PCs. More important, the company broadened its distribution to embrace the growing use of wireless services through a relationship with PageNet to provide pager users with wireless access to personalized content, Yahoo! Mail and Yahoo! Calendar.

In May 2000, a new partnership was announced with AT&T Wireless Services to provide a range of content and services for subscribers of its Digital PocketNet service, including news, mail, sports and finance. Under the plan, Yahoo! users will gain wireless access to personalized content delivered by two-way interactive services and notifications to the AT&T Internet-ready telephones.

It's obvious that Yahoo!'s leadership position in the business-to-consumer marketplace has been greatly supported through a large number of strategic business partnerships that have added a wide range of content and services for Yahoo! users and provided added value to its partners. And this partnership strategy will no doubt continue to play a key role as the company evolves.

But how the company can apply this partnership strategy to its new and probably most challenging initiative will attract even greater attention in the future.

## MAKING THE MOVE TO B2B

In June 2000, Yahoo! unveiled its intention to become a player in the enterprise information portal market by announcing development of Corporate Yahoo! This service, based on the company's popular My Yahoo! customizable interface, will allow companies to integrate proprietary corporate content and applications with Yahoo!'s personalized Internet content and services without going beyond their existing network firewalls.

It's definitely a strategic move, given the lucrative results that can be achieved from the business-to-business e-commerce marketplace. For example, analysts at Merrill Lynch predict that the enterprise information portal market, which represented $4.4 billion in 1998, will climb to more than $14.8 billion by 2002. Forrester Research, on the other hand, predicts even bigger potential, forecasting that B2B e-commerce will generate some $2.7 trillion by 2004.

It's no wonder that established business-to-consumer companies like Yahoo! are eyeing such a big pie. And unlike its early days, Yahoo! has a lot more competition at this stage of the game. Several other consumer-oriented companies have announced similar intentions, including AOL, About.com, NBCi and Beyond.com.

Analysts are skeptical as to whether or not these efforts will prove fruitful. "[These companies] face formidable challenges in obtaining business customers," Mitch Tuchman, a general partner at the B2B-focused venture capital firm Net Market Partners, told Redherring.com "It's hard to imagine what value [they] can add." (March 21, 2000.)

Some experts agree that any company whose revenue strategy is based on attracting large consumer audiences with content, and collecting advertising fees, will not make it in the B2B arena. Success comes only to those who have extensive domain experience and business relationships, that is, those who are already part of the supply chain of an industry.

Others, however, believe that companies such as Yahoo! can succeed given their established relationships with top businesses around the world. And, more important, that success can come only if they have solid partners to support their efforts. And Yahoo! is starting this B2B initiative with some pretty solid partnerships with leading technology and application service providers.

Corporate Yahoo! will utilize TIBCO Software's TIBCO Active-Portal and ActiveEnterprise product suites that companies can use to connect, integrate and automate their back-office and front-office applications to their portals, and then connect customers and partners to these systems via the Web. Inktomi, which originally provided search and navigation technology for Yahoo!'s other properties, now focuses solely on supporting Yahoo!'s enterprise portals with search capabilities for documents and information on corporate Intranets.

Other technology partnerships offer a wide variety of services for B2B customers. Using Citrix System's Nfuse technology, companies launch server-based applications from a standard Web page with the click of a mouse. Netegrity's SiteMinder secure management platform provides single sign-on, authentication management and entitlement management. Messaging and personal information management is supported by Critical Path's InLine resource management, InSchedule calendaring, InScribe email messaging and InScribe secure file services. And WebEx provides Web-conferencing and real-time meeting and video collaboration tools for interactive intranet conferencing.

# KEEP COMMUNITY IN MIND WHEN DEVELOPING PARTNERSHIPS

Yahoo! understands the importance of building successful partnerships with companies to obtain collaborative advantage, but it also extends that philosophy, through its Yahoo! Community Partners program, to not-for-profit organizations.

The company does not provide cash grants or financial sponsorships to these organizations. Rather, Yahoo! offers limited sponsorships of online media exposure to qualified nonprofit organizations to promote global community awareness through outreach, education and information access.

Why develop community partners? As the company notes in its Community Relations Guidelines: "By providing corporate resources to enduring organizations, we bring ideas and information to the forefront and enhance the vitality of our communities. Looking forward to the promise of the future is part of the corporate vision of Yahoo! And giving back to the community is an integral part of how we do business. This commitment is approached in the same way that drives the success of Yahoo!"

Other current Yahoo! partners are also expanding into this B2B initiative. Network Appliance, which currently provides storage capabilities for My Yahoo! and other properties, also services Corporate Yahoo! And Hewlett Packard will be the premier reseller, while also lending its expertise for sales, marketing, system integration and customer support.

Such a lengthy list of high-profile companies certainly will help make Corporate Yahoo! more appealing for prospective business customers, but Yahoo! does not stop there in terms of developing the right partnerships for this new venture.

To help overcome its lack of presence in the business-to-business marketplace, Yahoo! also partners with key players already established in the industrial-procurement arena. Dovebid, a major partner, is an 80-year-old capital assets auctioneer that has breathed new life into its business since re-launching as a bricks-and-click company in October 1999. In addition, Yahoo! works with Freemarkets (which acquired another key player Imark.com) and Tradeout.com to provide other industrial procurement services.

**Partnerships are not new to the business world, but they have become essential tools for success.**

Yahoo! believes that its ability to provide user-focused scalable and customized content and services on a global basis will effectively serve as a natural extension to corporate services. "We see a tremendous opportunity to fill the same needs for businesses that Yahoo! currently fills for the mass consumer audience," Mallet said in a company statement.

And, no doubt, its philosophy of partnering with the best – a strategy that moved the company from an Internet search engine to a leader in Internet communications, commerce and media – will remain a key building block to achieve success in the new market.

# PARTNERSHIPS CAN BE PROFITABLE

Partnerships are not new to the business world, but they have become essential tools for success. It's a fact of life: companies both large and small can't go it alone. Consumers demand so much more these days, and any company that thinks it can be all things to all people – and shuns the idea of partnering to achieve that goal – is destined to experience a harsh reality check down the road.

Yahoo! provides an excellent lesson in partnerships through its ability to weave partnerships throughout its dynamic business strategy. Its myriad relationships have allowed the company to expand its platform, extend its reach and build the brand.

If you believe that partnerships can be profitable for your business, you're halfway there. But much care must be given to the partnership process. Here are a few pointers you need to keep in mind:

◆ *To be the best, you must partner with the best.* Identify those businesses that have the best products or services that will provide the greatest added value to your products and services. Creating relationships just for the sake of adding "more stuff" will not achieve the true potential of partnerships. Take a hint from Yahoo! The majority of its partners achieved industry leadership, status and recognition well before relationships were made.

◆ *Partnerships are a two-way street.* It's important to continually keep your own needs in mind, but remember that the best partnerships are based on mutual need. Both sides must have something that the other needs and wants to achieve their respective business objectives. Any good relationship ultimately produces outcomes that benefit both partners.

◆ *Maintain a customer focus.* Successful partnerships must satisfy each other's needs, but it's customers who eventually give the thumbs up or thumbs down. Yahoo! pays careful attention to its users as a baseline to determine which new relationships it needs to create. Customer feedback proves essential in helping you to determine where you need to go and who you need to seek out.

◆ *Determine how a partnership can benefit your company.* You can't enter into any relationship without pinpointing exactly what both sides want the partnership to achieve. As we've seen with Yahoo!, its partnerships have achieved a variety of positive outcomes: expanded content offerings; additional online services; co-branded marketing opportunities; and greater distribution to attract new users. Many times, one partnership can achieve several positive outcomes. These need to be carefully thought out and defined during the relationship-building process.

◆ *Always keep the doors open.* Partnerships are created with defined strategies and expected outcomes, but opportunities often arise when you least expect them. Tunnelvision can kill. That's why each partnership from the start must recognize that twists and turns are inevitable on the business road. When an unexpected but potentially advantageous turn in the road appears, both sides must be flexible in their relationship to take it. If not, someone else will.

# REFERENCES

Moss Kanter, Rosabeth (1994) "Collaborative Advantage: The Art of Alliances," *Harvard Business Review*, July 1, 1994 p. 96.

Goldstein, Jon (1997) "Q&A: Yahoo! Is Worth $1.5 Billion. Insane? Jerry Yang Thinks Not," *Time*, November 1, 1997, pp. 30ff.

Anon. (2000) "Yahoo Wins Support for Its Independent Strategy," Reuters, January 12, 2000.

CNBC/Dow Jones (1998) Yahoo! CEO Interview, Christine Bushey, CNBC/Dow Jones Business Video, Interactive Desktop Video LLC, February 26, 1998.

Anon. (2000) "AOL and Yahoo! Get Down to Business," Herring Online, March 21, 2000.

Six

# BUY WHAT YOU NEED

Yahoo! excels at aggregating content and developing partnerships with key players on the Internet playing field as a way to grow its business. But is that enough to stay alive in the online jungle?

Often it's not. We've seen a number of industries over the years – from airlines to pharmaceuticals and everything in between – restructure themselves through mergers and acquisitions. And today's dot coms are proving to be no exception to inevitable consolidation in the landscape.

The merger of AOL and Time Warner set the Internet industry on its ear. Analysts were foaming at the mouth as they surveyed the market in search of the next big marriage. The spotlight, naturally, fell immediately on Yahoo! The grapevine was abuzz with rumors that the company couldn't help but make a similar move or risk losing strength in the fight with its closest rival. By spring 2000, word on the street had Yahoo! in merger talks with eBay, News Corp. and even Disney.

As we go to press, a marriage has not happened. Koogle, when asked outright on the Motley Fool Radio Show (April 18, 2000) about the eBay rumor, did his best corporate sidestep with the standard "we do not make comments on any kinds of rumors and speculations." Smart move, actually, when you realize that the company's competitors always have an ear glued to the ground.

Will Yahoo! ever make a move like AOL and gobble up another media outlet? It's tough to tell at this point. In many aspects it seems inevitable, given the way the industry and technology are changing. But it also seems unlikely, given Yahoo!'s previous track record and a penchant for all things Web-based.

At press time, analysts were noting that dot coms in critical condition were flocking in droves to Yahoo! and other solid Internet pillars. Therefore, the company no doubt will continue to acquire, probably at bargain-basement prices. But it's not as if Yahoo! hasn't been in the buyer's seat. In this chapter, we'll take a look at many of the key purchases Yahoo! has made to support its growth and expansion. After all, despite its wide range of alliances and agreements that fuel content and services, Yahoo! sometimes finds that it's better to buy it rather than partner with it.

# STRATEGY GUIDES
# THE SHOPPING CART

In several interviews Koogle has made no bones about Yahoo!'s constant eye for a good buy. But you can be sure that any acquisition undergoes an incredible amount of behind-the-scenes scrutiny guided by the strategy Yahoo! holds near and dear to its heart – creating the best Web experience possible.

"We have a filter that we lay on things," he explained during The Motley Fool interview. Such analysis, guided by its business strategy, determines whether or not a potential acquisition can truly expand on that strategy, provide faster time to market, fit into the existing culture or even work from a balance-sheet standpoint. As Koogle has said, we do the "normal process."

These are, in fact, the guidelines any company should use when scanning a potential buy. It's not an easy process, nor a fail-safe one. A majority of M&As have proven successful, but the corporate world is also littered with numerous examples of acquisitions gone wrong, even ones that seemed so promising at the outset. Therefore it's imperative to do your homework first – as Koogle says Yahoo! does – before jumping into a business marriage.

Let's take a look at some of Yahoo!'s purchases over the years and how they made it through Yahoo!'s filter process to become building blocks for the company's continued success.

## EAT THE COMPETITION

When you're hot, you know it and want to show it. Any company feeling its oats finds it hard to resist buying up a pesky competitor. It gives you a chance to flex a little muscle in the marketplace that can make others in your industry quake in their boots. And let's not forget attracting the eye of hot-to-trot investors who literally swoon at the sight of corporate muscle.

But it's the emotion-like appeal of these types of acquisitions that can get companies in trouble down the road. Power buying won't get you very far. As Koogle says, it's got to be a good fit. Take Yahoo!'s acquisition of Four11 Corporation in late 1997 as an example. At the time, Four11 had made a name for itself as creator of several directory services that included email, phone and address listings. It also developed Internet-based communications, such as net-phone software tools and RocketMail, which CNET ranked as the best free email at the time.

Yahoo! – which had recently launched its Yahoo! Mail service based on RocketMail technology – couldn't help but salivate over this opportunity. Four11's net-phone software offered an obvious extension of online communication services, and its directories complemented Yahoo!'s own chats, message boards, classifieds, yellow pages and white pages. Yahoo! said "Yum," and the marriage proved essential in its ability to leverage Four11's content and technologies into its network properties.

## Come together for commerce

By 1998, Yahoo! was feeling its oats even more in the shopping aisle, and two major acquisitions focused on generating strength in the commerce arena.

**Although initial success was gained from advertising revenue, the continued focus on online commerce never left Yahoo!'s sights.**

Although initial success was gained from advertising revenue, the continued focus on online commerce never left Yahoo!'s sights. Its merchant services had gained the support and attracted the dollars from leading companies throughout the world. Now the company wanted to offer similar services to small and midsize businesses. Enter ViaWeb.

ViaWeb Inc., a privately held company in Cambridge, MA, had built a name for itself by developing software and reporting tools for building and operating online-commerce Web sites. Its ViaWeb Store had been showered with numerous accolades and industry awards in 1997, including the Editor's Choice Award from *PC Magazine* and a four-star rating from *PC Computing* magazine. More than 1000 clients were already onboard the electronic store.

And Yahoo! put out the welcome mat with its purchase. Koogle said at the time that demand drove this acquisition. "We've had tremendous demand among businesses of all sizes to establish online stores and to secure distribution on Yahoo!," he was quoted in a company press release (June 8, 1998). What ViaWeb allowed Yahoo! to accomplish was to reach out even further into the business market for online merchants by using the buyout as the foundation for launching its Yahoo! Store full-service program that included setup, design, hosting and marketing support.

So it's no wonder that a mere four months later, Yahoo! hit the buyer trail again with its acquisition of Yoyodyne, a leading direct-marketing services firm founded by Seth Godin. The company had pioneered its own leading brands of custom direct marketing programs: EZSpree.com aggregated name-brand online shopping sites; GetRichClick.com analyzed site traffic to remove duplications and more closely target users; EZVenture.com, promoted specifically to entrepreneurs and small businesses; and EZWheels.com linked car buyers to manufacturers.

Yoyodyne, in fact, had really sharpened its skills in terms of successful online promotions, a resource that Yahoo! could not live without. By bringing it in-house, Yahoo! upped the ante for merchants in terms of providing them with more high-powered, targeted promotions within its arsenal.

But more important, absorbing Yoyodyne into the business signaled Yahoo!'s awareness of the growing trend toward one-to-one direct relationships with customers that the Web continued to fuel. It welcomed permission-based marketing into its culture (which we'll talk about more in Chapter 8), and gained an extensive database of consumers who had indicated their willingness to be approached. A big plus for Yahoo! merchant services ... and not bad for Yahoo!'s own business needs.

## GO FOR THE TECHNOLOGY FLOW

We all know the impact "new and improved" technology has on our own buying habits. When a new piece of software hits the market, and its capabilities and improved features catch our eye, we'll buy it, install it, and run with it. Sure beats the hell out of trying to write the software on our own.

Yahoo! is no different in its approach to new technology. And as we've noted earlier, it never considered itself a technology company from day one. So buying what you need in terms of technology continues to rule Yahoo!'s acquisitive mind.

The company started 1999 off with a bang in this respect when it announced the purchase of GeoCities. Started in 1994, GeoCities had pioneered development of Web-based communities by offering easy-to-use Web-based publishing tools. By the time Yahoo! came calling, GeoCities had created one of the largest online communities by hosting more than 3.5 million sites developed with its personal publishing tools. It achieved a stunning combined home/work reach of 33.4 percent at the time.

On the surface, the community-building philosophies appeared to be a match made in heaven. Two pioneering companies would join forces for the common good of the Internet world. Yet GeoCities – which represented Yahoo!'s biggest acquisition to date – had good leverage in its ability to bring personal publishing technology to the table.

And its established user base would prove to be a boon in expanding Yahoo!'s reach into the marketplace. The company noted in its announcement of January 28, 1999 that the addition of GeoCities to its network properties could create a combined, unduplicated home/work reach exceeding 58 percent. That would make it one of the largest network properties on the Web, second only to you-know-who.

Even better was the fact that GeoCities' community was built on self-published sites, or neighborhoods, which also included a wide collection of discussion groups. Integrating these neighborhoods into the Yahoo! network would help it overcome a problem Yahoo! was dealing with: short user time.

> When a new piece of software hits the market ... we'll buy it, install it, and run with it.

As Sajai Krishnan, a principal at the consulting firm Booz·Allen & Hamilton, told the Associated Press regarding the merger: "Yahoo's main limitation is that many people only use it for brief periods of time, something advertisers dislike." (*Dallas Morning News*, January 29, 1999.) "They're trying to keep people on their Web sites for as long as possible and give people as little opportunity as possible to leave."

Yahoo!, it seems, believed it was worth a hefty price for GeoCities – a 52 percent premium from its stock price despite the company's report that it lost $8.4 million, or 27 cents a share, on sales of $7.5 million during the previous quarter. Koogle was not sweating the issue. He obviously believed in the power of numbers. His response: "We are very comfortable with this premium. There is a competitive market for leading brands that a have a very large audience."

While focusing on building a larger audience that would stay longer on its network, Yahoo! never lost track of where the market was going in terms of media technology. Within four months, it announced yet another acquisition that would prove to signify a major milestone in the emergence of Web-based video content.

## NOW HEAR ... AND SEE ... THIS!

In a deal estimated to be worth $6 billion at that time, Yahoo! bought Broadcast.com, a leading aggregator and broadcaster of streaming audio and video programming. Despite facing bandwidth limitations in the marketplace, the company had attracted a stunning array of clients, including AT&T, Dell, Forbes, Harvard University, Intel and Microsoft.

Some observers praised the move as an affirmation that integration of traditional video and audio news, information and entertainment would transform Yahoo! into a media content giant. They claimed the acquisition could move Yahoo! to a new level of competition that could challenge the likes of Snap and Go Network that were partnering with such media giants as NBC and Disney. Others claimed that Yahoo! would focus on using Broadcast.com to strengthen its advertising resources and add greater appeal to advertisers by creating a rich media advertising distribution channel.

As it turned out, both sides were right.

Yahoo! knew that buying Broadcast.com would give it speed-to-market advantages for audio and video broadcasts, all part of its ongoing strategy to enhance user experiences. Content and business partners would both benefit from having a full turnkey audio and streaming video solution that, as research was uncovering, delivered deeper advertising impressions.

A 1998 study conducted by @Home found that rich media ads delivered over broadband made deeper impressions on consumers than narrowband, generating a 44 percent recall rate that was 34 percent better than recall rates for narrowband ads.

That's why the merger created Yahoo! Broadcast Services, which allowed Broadcast.com to continue working from its Dallas offices as a business unit and provide technical, operational and strategic direction in providing streaming content and services to network users and business services clients. It rolled seamlessly into Yahoo!'s sales organization as well.

At the same time, however, Yahoo! kept a vigilant eye on an evolving trend emerging from traffic statistics. In 1998, the company started seeing a shift in traffic patterns; more people were accessing their site from work, which also happened to be where the majority of high-speed lines existed. Yet Yahoo! had made its success in the narrowband arena, serving up Web pages designed to download fast for dial-up modem users.

As Koogle told *Fortune* in May 2000, "We said, 'Aha! That's an interesting asset.' We've got a broadband base that is way larger than anybody else's. And we can begin to serve them with things that we think are going to be compelling, which is seamless integration of text, fixed graphics and moving stuff – audio and video – all in one place." (*Fortune*, May 29, 2000.)

Broadband, in turn, was already indicating a tremendous impact on the future market. Cable operator MediaOne, for example, had sent out a team of anthropologists to study how broadband access affected families. What they saw proved amazing: families with high-speed access literally moved their PCs out of the den and into the living room. Computer usage skyrocketed an additional 18 hours a week, and family members who previously shunned computers started to surf.

An apparent shakeup seems inevitable. As Bruce Kassel, a senior analyst at Forrester Research, noted: "The skills of the portals need to change. They're going to have to become more adept at providing almost TV-like – and less computerlike – experiences." (*Fortune*, May 29, 2000.)

Given Yahoo!'s penchant for upgrading user experiences, Mallet and Koogle immediately began brainstorming on their vision of what a broadcast version of Yahoo! would look like. The first step proved relatively easy. They integrated Broadcast.com's broadband content from 400 radio stations, 450 sports teams and live or recorded press conferences and analysts meetings into its Web-based network.

The next step proved more challenging and only recently introduced at the time of writing. Yahoo!'s FinanceVision, officially launched on March 13, 2000, added a new tool to the company's already hugely successful finance site. A four-frame presentation includes streaming video for news anchor footage, links to additional information that change each time a different stock is named during the broadcast, and an area for the user's personal portfolio.

It's a work in progress, and it's difficult to say whether this will, in fact, turn Yahoo! into a media content behemoth. But it's also an incredible glimpse into the potential future for Yahoo!, one that co-founder Jerry Yang has said will not focus solely on one platform or bandwidth strategy.

Even though more than half of Yahoo!'s 120 million users were accessing them through broadband pipes by the end of 1999, Yang believes that other means to access content and services cannot be pushed aside. That's why Yang did not seem worried about the AOL/Time Warner merger when he talked to *Fortune*: "We're going to focus on delivering high-quality, easy-to-use broadband content services and applications on the Internet, regardless of platform, device or what other kind of access you use. If you have the bandwidth and you consume it, we'll have a service for you."

# KEEP THOSE COMMUNICATIONS COMING

Yang wasn't kidding. Even as its FinanceVision program was launching, Yahoo! was heading toward another acquisition designed to enhance its communication services. In June 2000, the company announced its intention to purchase eGroups, a widely used email group communication platform. With more than 17 million members who have created more than 80,000 active email groups, the company also brings with it additional features such as group calendars, file sharing, polling and email archives. All of these, naturally, will be spun into its established Yahoo! Mail, Yahoo! Clubs and Yahoo! Messenger services.

Both sides praised this latest merger as a big step toward developing the world's largest, user-friendly and comprehensive group communications platform. But, given the additional capabilities brought to the Yahoo! arsenal, the combination no doubt will also play a key role in supporting the development of communications services for Corporate Yahoo! we mentioned in Chapter 5.

## Tips for smart shoppers

At the rate companies buy each other up these days, business acquisitions often seem almost matter-of-fact. Nothing could be further from the truth. The purchasing process is extensive in terms of time, effort and money. And it revolves around four key questions that must be carefully thought out and answered positively before any deal is reached:

◆ *Will it expand our business strategy?* Let's be real here: any company that buys another firm solely as a trophy it can showcase will in the long run lose in the deal. Sure, it's tempting for market leaders to snatch up competitors as a means to command more control. But such muscle flexing won't prevent new threats from emerging on the horizon. The best purchases, therefore, are guided by the strategies that have elevated a company to the point where it can sit in the buyer's seat. As we've seen with Yahoo!, its buying patterns are guided by the fact that they only buy Web-based assets. Makes sense, after all, since their business has always been the Web. That's why its purchases of Four11 and Broadcast.com made such sense. The directory service and the broadband multimedia company were natural fits with Yahoo!'s business model. But others, like AOL's purchase of Time Warner, were made on the belief that purchasing off-line – and online – assets is critical in supporting the business mission for content and services.

# YAHOO!'S BUYING GUIDE

If you haven't already noticed by now, a major theme runs through all of the acquisitions we've noted in this chapter.

Yes, each purchase allowed Yahoo! to expand existing services, provided quick time-to-market for new technologies, and built an even bigger audience to support its advertisers and business partners. The company – always keeping strategic vision in the forefront of its buying patterns – knows what it needs to buy to keep it competitive and attractive as a leading Internet communications, commerce and media player.

But there's also another factor coming into play here. And it reveals Yahoo!'s strong belief in all things Web-based. They do not purchase off-line assets. Every purchase to date has been of companies that deal strictly with Web-based technology and services. Yahoo! prefers to look for more clicks, not bricks.

As Koogle put it so succinctly during an appearance on the CNBC/ Dow Jones Business cable show *Street Signs* in May 1999, the company has no intention of purchasing what he called "off-line assets."

But don't get us wrong. Yahoo! does not stick its nose up at brick-and-mortar companies. That would be foolish, since they represent a big reason why Yahoo! became successful in the first place. Those who operate both on and off the Web still represent a major part of Yahoo!'s ongoing business strategy, but not in terms of business acquisitions.

As Koogle put it: "We're mostly focused on continuing to build our Web-based franchise and do great business with companies that also operate off the Web for cross promotion ... but in business deals."

◆ *Will it get us to market faster?* No doubt about it. When it comes to business, there is a constant need for speed. Internal changes and improvements are crucial in a dynamic marketplace, but they may not happen within the timeframe you need. Acquisitions, therefore, can quickly move you further into established markets or give you fast entrance into new markets. Take Yahoo!'s purchases of ViaWeb and GeoCities, as examples. GeoCities offered Yahoo! better tools that enhanced an already established core competency – online community development. ViaWeb, on the other hand, gave Yahoo! a technological leg-up to move quickly into a new arena of providing online shopping services for small and mid-size businesses. A decision to buy, therefore, must be predicated on the fact that assets gained will move you much faster than any internal efforts could ever achieve.

◆ *Does it fit into our existing culture?* This is such an important aspect of business acquisitions, but many experts will tell you that it's also the aspect most overlooked in the process. Two opposing cultures will have the same effect as mixing oil and water. Ask those who suffered through such megamergers as Ford and Volvo or Bell Atlantic and GTE, to name but two. Despite the fact that a potential purchase may look extremely appealing in terms of business strategy and faster time-to-market, all mergers inevitably involve people. And conflicts that arise within the human capital of companies can quickly prevent those benefits from coming to fruition. The reality is, cultural conflicts are almost impossible to avoid. Companies rarely have cookie-cutter cultures that merge easily into one. But knowing the challenges upfront and being prepared to face them once the purchase takes place will help to support your return on investment.

◆ *Does it work from a balance-sheet standpoint?* Indeed, the entire transaction must be viable from a bottom-line perspective. That's why every potential purchase must undergo thorough due diligence before a deal is cemented. But numbers on a spreadsheet alone cannot guide the buying decision. They do, however, provide the final piece in this "filter" process, as Koogle calls it, which determines whether or not to move forward. If you're sure that the purchase can support your business strategy, provide you with the speed you need, and eventually work from a cultural standpoint, then a good balance sheet analysis will give you the complete confidence you need as a smart shopper.

# REFERENCES

Kalish, David & Knox, Noelle (1999) "Yahoo! to buy GeoCities for $5 billion," *Dallas Morning News*, January 29, 1999.

Roth, Daniel (2000) "Surprise! Yahoo Goes Broadband," *Fortune*, May 29, 2000, Vol. 141, No. 11, pp 182ff.

Gardner, David and Gardner, Tom (2000) Fool Interview with Tim Koogle, chairman and CEO of Yahoo!, The Motley Fool Radio Show, April 18, 2000.

Haines, Mark (1999) Street Signs: Yahoo! CEO Interview, CNBC/Dow Jones Business Video, Interactive Desktop Video LLC, March 1, 1999.

Seven

# BRAND IT!

# YAHOO!

The company behind the name did not, in fact, coin the term. That credit goes to Jonathan Swift who invented the word with the publication of his classic tale *Gulliver's Travels* in 1726. You may recall that Gulliver travels to Houyhnmhnmland. Its rulers – the Houyhnmhnm – are a refined, sensitive and highly ethical people who also happen to be horses. While there, the story's hero also encounters the Yahoos, who are savage and ape-like in appearance. Swift described them as possessing the worst of human vices – cunning, malicious and treacherous, yet basically cowards.

Swift's depiction of the Yahoos made a quite an impact, and the word almost immediately entered the English language as a term to describe a moronic, loudmouthed and sometimes violent hooligan. In more recent times, modern society adopted the word to describe someone as unrefined or lacking culture. As Funk & Wagnalls notes as its secondary definition, a "bumpkin."

We noted earlier in this book that the co-founders of Yahoo! reportedly selected this word for their company because they felt it best described themselves personally in relation to the new Internet frontier. But they did, in a way, make the word their own by adding the exclamation mark as part of their corporate trademark.

An interesting and surely memorable company moniker, we agree. But selecting such an interesting corporate signature proved only part of its success. What's even more fascinating is the way that Yahoo! has turned its off-beat identifier into one of the most recognized brands ever to arise from the Internet.

## BRANDING FROM THE BEGINNING

Yang and Filo knew from the start that what they had as a business was a brand. As Yang told *Time* in 1997, that insight was evident to them as they wrote their first business plan in August of 1995. "We knew that we weren't going to be a technology company," he recalled. "What we had was a brand."

One of their first smart moves in brand building was to hire a respected public-relations crew that already had gained experience in this very new medium.

But realization, as they say, is only half the battle. The co-founders faced a major undertaking in building their search engine into an established brand that would stand out in the fast-exploding Internet arena. This was virgin territory in terms of business development, and the Stanford graduate students knew they couldn't make it happen on their own.

One of their first smart moves in brand building was to hire a respected public-relations crew that already had gained experience in this very new medium. Yang and Filo signed up with the Niehaus Ryan Group – now known as Niehaus Ryan Wong Inc. (NWR) – in 1995. The firm was one of the first agencies at the time to recognize the Internet as a potentially powerful marketplace and was working hard to create awareness by routinely inviting journalists to their offices to surf the Web. More important, the agency had hands-on experience with Internet marketing, having worked with GNN and Spry to create Internet in a Box.

Such Internet-savvy expertise was rare at the time, and no doubt costly to boot. As struggling startup entrepreneurs, Yang and Filo were naturally strapped for cash. They did, however, manage to gain the agency's services through a creative payment arrangement that included one part cash and one part stock.

Such a deal was unique at the time, and certainly a gamble. But as Blaise Simpson, the agency's Yahoo! account manager told *Red Herring* magazine: "Of course, the stock probably turned out to be a much better deal with us." (January 1998.) So much so, that the agency used similar arrangements with other struggling startups later on.

> As struggling startup entrepreneurs, Yang and Filo were naturally strapped for cash. They did, however, manage to gain the agency's services through a creative payment arrangement that included one part cash and one part stock.

Bringing top talent on board was certainly a key to begin the building of its brand, but Yahoo! also was smart enough to plug into that talent at a strategic time. As many brand-management gurus will tell you, it's important for companies to give themselves adequate time for discussion and planning before a commercial launch. And many note that most companies are johnny-come-latelies in this respect.

NWR co-founder and president Ed Niehaus is one of those gurus. As he told *UPSIDE Magazine* (May 6, 1999): "People should talk to PR agencies much earlier than they think," adding that he could name a litany of other clients that have knocked on his agency's door a mere month or so before a commercial launch. And when such short-notice campaigns fail to make a media splash, the finger usually points to the PR doctors.

Having adequate time for planning allows companies and their PR strategists to work through what NWR calls its "Architecture of Identity," a service it developed in late 1998 for high-tech and interactive media companies based on its previous successes in building brands for Yahoo! and other high-profile Internet firms, such as CyberCash and Marimba. Using a process that incorporates competitive research, executive workshops and strategic brainstorming sessions, the result is an overall "identity framework" which companies use as a benchmark for all corporate and product communications. The goal: moving outside the box of traditional brand thinking.

# THE ELEMENTS OF BRAND-BUILDING

But it's the interplay among three factors behind brand identity that ultimately prove key to creating a sustainable identity in a fast-changing marketplace:

◆ *Vision* – why does your company exist, and where is it going in the future?

◆ *Positioning* – where do you stand in customers' minds in relation to the competition?

◆ *Voice* – what type of personality do you want to communicate?

As we noted earlier, the vision of Yahoo!'s co-founders was pretty much in place right from the start. They did not set out to be a tech company. Rather, they saw the Internet as a chaotic medium and believed their success would come from developing a gateway that would provide user-friendly services and comprehensive content that would make sense out of the exploding online arena.

As Yang said in 1997, "We will continue to position ourselves as a place where people can look for information and product services, and where merchants can reach these consumers. As long as we keep ourselves in that gateway position, we will be in good shape."

One year later, Karen Edwards, Yahoo!'s director of brand management, supported that continued vision when she explained the company's brand message to *Red Herring*: "Yahoo! is an Internet media company, not just a search engine. The press is finally starting to realize that Yahoo! hasn't changed. The market has matured, so perceptions of us have changed."

Although the vision remained steadfast, the company's strategies regarding positioning have changed over the years. As Niehaus recalled, the first strategic meeting with Yahoo! focused on positioning. At that time, the company and its PR firm agreed that Yahoo! would be positioned as a Web directory, not a search engine. "We wanted to evangelize about how the Internet would change people's lives," he noted, adding that Yahoo!'s decision not to be viewed as a technology made it positively "allergic" to the term "search engine."

# BRAND BECOMES "SHOW"

Yahoo!'s anti-technology strategy was indeed a shrewd move at the time, given the fact that the Internet was still in its infancy and a majority of consumer households had yet to go online. At the same time, few journalists were actually covering the Internet on a regular basis. So an emphasis on consumer orientation created the first "voice" for Yahoo!, which quickly transformed into the "Dave Filo and Jerry Yang show."

NRW introduced Yahoo! to the world as the creation of two whiz kids from Stanford University. According to Bill Ryan, NRW co-founder and board chairman, the idea was to promote Filo and Yang as the embodiment of the energy and entrepreneurship that was fueling the Internet explosion. The two presented a very folksy – a kind of "aw-shucks-anybody-can-use-us" – image. It was a calculated approach, one developed to make the Internet – and more importantly Yahoo! – more accessible to the general public. It also helped the company to break out of the pack of existing competitors, such as Excite Inc., which actually had more sophisticated Web-based search engine software.

The marketing team pitched these stories not to the traditional tech trade and business publications but rather to mainstream consumer publications and lifestyle sections of newspapers, which jumped at the chance to spotlight the Internet wunderkinds. Within six months after launching its initial strategy, the company had collected some 600 articles.

# TIME TO GROW UP

Despite the success of its initial brand-building strategy, a major change was needed in early 1996. Yahoo! was nearing its deadline to go public, and its folksy image could actually be a liability in convincing the business world that the company was a solid investment. As Ryan noted, investors would not be too keen on investing a lot of money in a "bunch of kids running around the office without their shoes on." The emphasis shifted to promoting capable and experienced business management. The business press was courted heavily prior to the IPO.

As Edwards also recalled, Yahoo! needed to present itself as a grown-up and serious company. It had to prove that its business model was a feasible one. "We needed to convince the press that advertising on the Internet was a viable business," she said.

As we've talked about earlier in this book, Yahoo!'s IPO was a record-breaking event for the time. But the powers behind the company's brand-building strategy knew that success could be a killer. The IPO generated an unwieldy amount of hype that could literally act as a ball-and-chain for the company's continued success. The strategy changed once again.

According to Edwards, Yahoo! wanted to distance itself from the glamour of the IPO and focus more on the fact that the company was now in the Internet media business for the long haul. They turned to television advertising, a move that many observers believe was yet another savvy shift in creating a sustainable brand.

But Yahoo! did not completely forsake its consumer orientation, nor did it forget that entertainment would continue to play a major role in its content and related services. In 1996, Edwards enlisted the help of the Wasserman Group, a Los-Angeles-based, entertainment-oriented PR agency. The firm had a stunning client list that included such high-powered celebrities as the Beatles and the Rolling Stones. To the untrained eye, this match would seem more like oil and water, but as Edwards has explained, the reason was to support the consumer side of the business. With the continued launch of Yahoo! communities, she knew that these sites often appealed to more entertainment-minded individuals. NRW had the high-tech contacts, and Wasserman could complement the strategy with Hollywood connections.

That same year, Yahoo! also hired a boutique advertising agency, Black Rocket, to craft a campaign that could build on the awareness created by the IPO. Yes indeed, the company that had built success and revenues on selling advertising had decided to begin advertising itself on television. And it would be the first Internet company to do so.

The selection of Black Rocket was certainly a smart choice. As many observers have noted, this agency knew what many others in the business failed to recognize: that Yahoo! was a consumer brand, not a technology company. Therefore, the targeted market encompassed people who intended to go online, which IntelliQuest estimated that year to be roughly 18 million by 1998. The agency knew that experienced Web surfers remained quite loyal to their search engines, so the campaign needed to grab the attention of novice Internet users.

Even better, the agency grabbed hold of Yahoo!'s irreverent corporate personality that proved successful in the early days of its brand-building efforts. It pitched a new tag line: "Do You Yahoo!?" The company bought it, and the tongue-in-cheek TV ads began appearing on news shows and programs that appealed to a computer-savvy audience, including *The Late Show with David Letterman*, *Saturday Night Live* and *Star Trek*.

As Edwards told the *Minneapolis Star Tribune* (April 1996): "We're targeting information gatherers and people who are similar to the people we know are on the Net. We've done research and looked at the types of shows that have the most Web sites and Internet discussion activity."

The investment, as Edwards saw it, was well worth it. "It made us seem more established," she told *Red Herring*.

## THE BRAND EXPANDS

"Established" is probably an understatement. The strategy put Yahoo! at the top of the heap.

The brand-building strategy paid off big time in terms of loyalty that continues to fuel incredible increases in online traffic. By 1997, a survey by NPD Online Research Group ranked Yahoo! as having the highest levels of user satisfaction (92 percent rated the service as "excellent" or "very good") and loyalty (among all Web users surveyed, 29 percent said they used Yahoo! the most often, as compared with 17 percent who preferred AltaVista or 14 percent who liked Web Crawler).

At the time of this publication, Yahoo! continues to hold a strong following among Web users. Results from Media Metrix for July 2000 indicated that the Yahoo! network ranked third among the combined US home and work user audience. On the other hand, Nielsen//NetRatings placed it on top of the five leading Web sites worldwide both in terms of user traffic and average combined time spent by home and work users, which was slightly more than one hour during June 2000.

Such mind-boggling numbers can certainly be attributed to Yahoo!'s brand-building efforts that have turned it into a powerful marketing machine today. Success comes from its ability to target three different audiences using a distinct message for each one. As we noted earlier, the brand building began with a wink toward novice online consumers that promoted the brand as fun, easy to use and even a little wacky. As it matured, Yahoo! then embraced the business community with an image of professionalism and management expertise. Add to that, its continued message to media buyers that Yahoo! is the market leader in online advertising.

> As it matured, Yahoo! ... embraced the business community with an image of professionalism and management expertise.

And Yahoo! leverages that brand extensively on a multitude of fronts. It has licensed its name on a variety of products ranging from Ziff-Davis' *Yahoo! Internet Life* magazine, to snowboards. The company has entered into co-branded products, services and contests – which we'll look at more closely in the next chapter – with such other well-regarded brands as Ben & Jerry's, Visa and MCI. Now it will use its brand muscle to help it enter a totally new market with its Yahoo! Corporate services we discussed in Chapter five.

# SECRETS TO BRAND BUILDING

You cannot build a successful brand without keeping these
three fundamental elements in mind:

◆ *Always keep your vision in sight.* We know the term's over-
played. But in all honesty we can't think of a better way to
say it. Vision stands as a vital component for brand success.
Yahoo! has never lost sight of the fact that it is an Internet
media company, not a technology company. That's the
reason why it started, and it continues to be a force behind
its continued success. Companies that lose sight of why
they're in business in the first place too often jeopardize the
strength of their brands. After all, if a business isn't sure
exactly why it exists, its customers certainly won't be.

◆ *Position yourself against the competition.* Knowing who or what
you are is one thing, but customers need to know where
you stand in relation to the competition. In Yahoo!'s case, it
could have easily fallen into the trap of positioning itself as
a search engine. Search engines were indeed hot properties
at the time it launched, but the company knew its future
was more than just pointing people to other Web sites. And
that's the message it communicated – and still does – to Web
users. Consider how the site AskJeeves.com presents itself
as "the world's first Internet butler," not a search engine.
Your message must meet the same objectives: define for
your customers exactly who you are and how you differ from
the rest of the pack.

◆ *Speak in the best voice.* It's all about personality, and Yahoo!
certainly has personality. You see it in their ads, you hear it
in the messages they communicate. Visit style maven Martha

Stewart's home page and her name literally pops up all over it, from Martha by Mail to marthasflowers. True, your voice may need to change somewhat depending on the market you're approaching. Yahoo! has understood this fact over the years as it introduced itself to the consumer, investment and business worlds. The key is to make sure you're speaking in a voice that the audience wants and expects to hear.

## HOW TO BUILD YOUR BRAND

As the story of Yahoo! brand building attests, creating a sustainable brand requires the ability to know how to "balance your core identity" while understanding the need for "perpetual makeovers." This advice comes from William Ryan, the man who helped Yahoo! become what it is today.

Kenneth Roberts, CEO of Lippincott & Margulies, a New York-based, corporate brand identity management consulting firm, concurs. "Companies need to reinvent themselves on a nearly continuous basis or risk losing relevancy to the marketplace," he told *American Banker* (August 16, 1999). In this light, any appearance of stability can become a liability. Customers today want innovation, speed and ease of access. That requires all companies to increasingly look at new markets, new products and brand extensions to meet these expectations if they want to achieve continued growth and success.

Yahoo! serves as a classic example of this strategy. Take a look at the myriad of press releases on their corporate Web pages and you'll see that innovations, new products and brand extensions have played – and no doubt will continue to play – a key role in maintaining its leadership.

Also keep in mind that strong brands are created through more than just strong advertising campaigns. Yes, they do play a role, as Yahoo!'s case study can attest. But there are a few other tricks you should keep in mind when developing a brand-building strategy:

◆ *Give away the store!* No, not literally. However, distribution of free samples has been a staple for brand building among consumer products. But Internet companies take this to new heights by providing valuable services and content for free. Why? The goal is to quickly create affinity groups to your brand. Sounds like a money-losing proposition, doesn't it? Well, consider this quip from Anil Gadre, vice-president of worldwide marketing for Sun Microsystems: "You know what URL stands for? Ubiquity first, Revenues later." (*Fortune*, June 22, 1998, pp.167ff.) Also look at how AOL – who many consider to be the Godzilla of giveaways – built its brand by distributing free disks and offering one-month free trial services.

◆ *When it comes to public relations, it's war!* Giving away free stuff is great, but certainly not worthwhile when nobody knows about it. Yahoo! excelled at this, first working the celebrity marketing of its founders in the consumer press and then promoting management skills and expertise with the business press. High-profile events or marketing stunts, which Yahoo! also excels at, become key to getting the word out. Also consider the effectiveness of lobbying for important industry issues as a means to generate additional, positive brand building.

◆ *Make the Web work for you.* True, Yahoo! started as an Internet company, so the Web was its first marketplace. And it worked

# WHY BUILD A BRAND?

Although companies like Yahoo! seem to build incredibly strong brands almost overnight, the truth is that such brand-building efforts take sustained effort and investment. But the payoff can come in many ways because a strong brand will:

◆ allow you to charge premium pricing or achieve greater market share at the same price;

◆ differentiate your product and eliminate barriers to entering new markets;

◆ give you a strong platform on which to launch new products;

◆ improve customer loyalty and retention;

◆ enhance employee morale and pride in the company;

◆ support the ability to recruit top talent;

◆ make your business more attractive to potential business partners; and

◆ drive shareholder value.

(Source: *American Banker*, August 16, 1999.)

it well long before the TV ads started popping up. The key, however, is not to focus solely on the Web as an advertising vehicle. Consider the fact that some of the most popular sites, including Yahoo!, have succeeded because they provide extensive customer interaction and personalization. Tailoring the Web site to each customer's specific needs – as also seen with Amazon.com, CDNow and others – certainly supports brand loyalty. But such interaction also serves as an incredible customer communication tool as well. Yahoo! offers users a variety of ways to interact with each, but it also listens to what users say to them as well in terms of satisfaction and future expectations.

◆ *Have some fun!* Yahoo! has always been irreverent in its brand building, using funny advertising and even bizarre marketing stunts such as promoting online commerce during a parachute jump (see the next chapter for more on that one!) to support its brand. Sun has maintained a similar fun approach, particularly in its Java campaign. By creating its mascot Duke – part penguin and part tooth – it used the creature to promote Java as a tool to keep the Internet safe for everyone. It even created an entire comic book for software developers that prominently featured the lovable-looking mascot. And remember, being too serious can create missed opportunities. Take, for example, the incident a few years back when a prankster smashed a pie into the face of Microsoft's Bill Gates as he was heading to deliver a speech. Many observers believe Microsoft could have scored some major points if Gates had reacted differently and had had some fun with the incident.

# REFERENCES

"Yahoo, the evolution of an Internet startup's PR strategy," *Red Herring*, January 1998.

O'Brien, Tia (1999) "Naked Business: Secrets of Spin," *UPSIDE Today*, May 6, 1999.

Anon. (1996) "Yahoo to begin TV ad campaign to promote service," *Minneapolis Star Tribune*, April 26, 1996, pp. 3D.

Knapschaefer, Johanna (1999) "Identity Management," *American Banker*, August 16, 1999.

Nakache, Patricia (1998) "Smart Managing/Best Practices: Secrets of the New Brand Builders," *Fortune*, June 22, 1998, pp. 167ff.

Bergstrom, Alan (1999) "Promises and Expectations: Good Branding Requires Tapping into Functional and Emotional Needs," *American Banker*, August 16, 1999.

Wong, Neihaus Ryan (1998) Neihaus Ryan Wong's "Architecture of Identity" Translates into Brand Action, company release, November 9, 1998.

Eight

# PROMOTE THE HELL OUT OF IT

# YAHOO! EVERYWHERE

As a global Internet media company, Yahoo! certainly has made its presence known around the world through development of 23 community properties that now comprise its network. And the strategy continues from a technology standpoint as Yahoo! begins to permeate every corner of the electronically-enabled world through wireless accessibility for hand-held devices and TV-based Internet appliances, voice functionality and business-to-business services.

That's why the company continues to remain the darling of Wall Street. During its second analyst day on May 18, 2000, the Yahoo! Everywhere strategy continued to receive strong support and kudos from top financial analysts. Harry Blodget from Merrill Lynch, for example, lauded the company's strategy as a key factor for future success. "We believe the company remains exceptionally well-positioned to benefit from the Internet's impact on the global media, communications and commerce industries over the next several years." (NewsTraders Inc., May 19, 2000.)

But Yahoo!'s omnipresence in the marketplace also stems from its marketing prowess. It's a marketing machine that, as we discussed in the previous chapter, has been able to build a very strong brand. And it's a valuable one at that – worth some $2.89 billion – second only to America Online's $3.47 billion brand value, according to a valuation ranking from

Charlotte, NC-based Addison Whitney. (*Marketing Briefs, Marketing Educator,* June 22, 1998)

To be successful, however, Yahoo! really had no choice but to create a powerful marketing machine. After all, the company built itself as a content aggregator fueled by online advertising revenue. It had to support the marketing needs of its advertisers, and Yahoo! continues to provide an integrated set of sales and marketing tools through its Fusion Marketing service for nearly 3600 clients, including some of the most respected brands and advertising agencies in the world.

**Yahoo! has been quite aggressive in co-promoting its brand with a number of its clients through contests, special events, sponsorships and distribution arrangements.**

That support truly has paid off for Yahoo!, which proudly cites an *Advertising Age* survey that ranks the network as "Best Advertising Environment" among advertising and marketing directors. The company also claims a 90 percent contract renewal and extension rate among its advertising clients.

And Yahoo! has been quite aggressive in co-promoting its brand with a number of its clients through contests, special events, sponsorships and distribution arrangements. From sporting and entertainment events to charity campaigns, its name continually surfaces.

From its own corporate promotional standpoint, Yahoo! has made its way into just about every possible venue: from the streets of New York City to San Francisco taxi cabs; in television ads and radio spots; on race cars as well as Volkswagen; literally in the air and even tattooed on employees' body parts. In short, its aggressive marketing and promotional campaigns are the reason why people who don't even use the Internet most often recognize the name, even if they don't know exactly what the company does for a living.

## TREAT THE CUSTOMER WITH RESPECT

As aggressive as the company is with its marketing strategies, it has been careful not to take out such aggressions in other areas. As Yang noted early on during a keynote address at the Web Developer 1996 conference: 'It's a fine line delivering what the user can use and overcommercializing the Web." (Newsbyte News Network, February 14, 1996.) That's a big reason why Yahoo! champions Internet privacy and anti-spamming efforts while shunning in-your-face techniques. Instead, it created My Yahoo! personalization and embraced the trend of "permissions" marketing to create and manage relationships with its users.

It seems almost like a Jekyll and Hyde syndrome, and the company has had its share of critics who over the years claimed Yahoo! was missing the boat on one-to-one marketing and would suffer from it. But the balance continues to work well for the company, as we'll discuss further in this chapter.

## NOTHING BEATS A GOOD STORY ...

As we noted in the previous chapter, brand building has served as the cornerstone for Yahoo!'s marketing strategies from its earliest days. The first promotional wave focused on telling the "whiz-kids" story of Yahoo!'s co-founders. After all, it was a good story to tell and that is one aspect of successful marketing that can't be beat, according to Jerry Weissman, a former novelist and TV producer who later consulted for Yahoo! on its IPO marketing strategy.

But the story wasn't the right one to tell as the company was going public. That's why Weissman helped to refocus the story by emphasizing the experienced management team that Yahoo! had assembled during the year. "There's only one story an IPO audience wants to hear: Why is your company an attractive investment opportunity?" Weissman told *Fast Company* (June 1997).

Solid management, indeed, adds to a company's appeal, and Weissman credits Koogle's handling of some tricky questions during what he calls the "IPO road show" as a factor behind Yahoo!'s jaw-dropping public offering. CEOs on any such road show inevitably are asked what keeps them up at night. As Weissman noted, the best strategy is to admit what your problems are and then explain exactly what you're doing about them.

"Tim Koogle did that particularly well," Weissman recalled. "When Yahoo! went out, it was competing with four or five other search engine companies. Koogle responded to his audience's concerns by stressing the importance of brand identity. He talked about creating an image rather than a service." By doing so, Weissman added that Koogle preemptively answered the underlying question: why is Yahoo! different?

## ... BUT OVERHYPE CAN KILL

As much as any company would like to make a big splash in the marketplace almost overnight, it can't stray from an ancient rule of marketing: brands with staying power are not built overnight. Coke and Disney hammered out their brand strategies over several decades to achieve the top-brand recognition and loyalty they enjoy today. Any company flying high from an IPO as successful as Yahoo!'s can easily fall prey to believing it has achieved so rapidly what other companies take years to create.

Yahoo! understood that hype could kill when not properly managed, and it came face-to-face with that prospect on that day in April 1996 when it went public. As Neihaus recalled, reporters descended on the company like locusts in the hopes of getting exclusive coverage of the wild IPO. Rather than allow the spin of the record-breaking IPO to continue out of control, Yahoo! shut the doors on the media and refused to allow anyone inside the company's small Santa Clara offices. The reason: lawyers feared lawsuits from investors alleging that the stock did not live up to the hype.

> Yahoo! understood that hype could kill when not properly managed, and it came face-to-face with that prospect … when it went public.

A smart move, given the stock's performance in the days ahead. But, as Yahoo!'s director of brand management has said, the hype forced the company to change its story once again in an effort to distance itself from the "glamour" of the IPO and focus on its long-term commitment to business growth. And even during this stage, Yahoo! knew that the story had to be controlled at all times.

"As the company grows, managing spokespeople also becomes more challenging," Edwards told *Red Herring*, noting that

Yahoo!'s wide range of partnerships doesn't allow it to monitor all information. "It's difficult to control the information in our partners' press releases," she added.

But Yahoo! did look at itself internally and decided to support spin control by developing a training program for its employees on how to work with the press. "Because many of our employees are young and inexperienced, we have to train them to become media savvy very quickly, so they won't spill confidential information to the press," according to Edwards.

> Yahoo! did look at itself internally and decide to support spin control by developing a training program for its employees on how to work with the press.

Growth continues to be leading concern for Yahoo!'s marketing strategy. And as Edwards has advised, any company's ongoing story must reflect that issue. "A company has to think about where it's going to be in a couple of years," she said. That becomes key in hiring the right public relations support because, as she noted, the agency must be able to take the company to where it wants to go.

## GETTING OFF THE GROUND

Hype is one thing, but having fun is another. And Yahoo!'s marketing campaigns offer some valuable examples of how to create attention without losing sight of strategic objectives. The Yahoo! Everywhere mantra weaves its way through a number of promotional efforts – even stunts – to constantly hammer home its message.

Probably one of its more unique promotions occurred at the start of the 1999 holiday shopping season. Yahoo! had some news it wanted to share: its online commerce services had achieved record-breaking volumes on "Black Friday," the Friday following Thanksgiving known as one of the busiest shopping days of the year. Transactions on Yahoo! Shopping had increased 400 percent from the same day the previous year. The company proudly waved its record transaction volume as clear evidence that consumers were embracing the convenience of online shopping.

Now Yahoo! could have left it at that, and probably gained plenty of positive press coverage from its sales figures as indicators of consumer confidence in online transactions. But the company bundled this bright bit of news into a fun campaign that showcased new wireless capabilities. In short, Yahoo! reached new heights in its "Everywhere" strategy by conducting a new and innovative approach to the old cliché "shop 'til you drop" – the world's first mid-air online purchase. As a skydiver (provided by Extreme Video Productions) descended towards Stanford Stadium from 7000 feet using a Yahoo!-branded parachute, he logged into Yahoo! Shopping using a touch-screen computer (supplied by NEC) with a wireless modem (provided by Business Tel). Within 45 seconds, he purchased a Spring Air Infinity mattress and safely landed on the field's 50-yard line.

Although not as dramatic, several other marketing campaigns still fit perfectly into the Yahoo! Everywhere strategy. Earlier in 1999, it rolled out "the world's first taxi fortified with Yahoo!" A logo-laden purple and yellow taxi, co-sponsored by Luxor Cab Company and the City of San Francisco Taxicab Commission, hit the streets of the Bay Area, providing riders with mobile access to Yahoo! services at no additional charge. This campaign continued to play on the fact that even people "on the go" could use its services.

Even the streets of New York City could not be spared the presence of Yahoo! As part of the city's popular public art exhibit CowParade 2000, Yahoo! provided what it called "the first-ever Internet connected cows" to showcase its email services by presenting Yahoo! Moo Mail. These two cow-shaped kiosks, powered by Lexitech's NetKey Internet and Secure Enterprise software, allowed residents and tourists to browse the Web, check email via Yahoo! Mail accounts, and access additional information about the CowParade throughout the summer.

## Getting a good buzz

Never afraid to have a little pun-filled fun in its marketing efforts, Yahoo!'s executions receive kudos from marketing gurus for adhering to its strategic vision while showcasing fun and innovative approaches to create the "buzz."

According to Michael Krauss, partner at Diamond Technology Partners, a Chicago-based e-commerce consulting firm, there are several secrets to successful marketing that create the kind of "buzz" you need. These include selecting the right venues, setting clear objectives, creating synergies and presenting creative and edgy events (*Marketing News*, May 22, 2000). These types of campaigns may look and feel more like parties, but the business purpose is never neglected. And the best ones achieve multiple ends with multiple audiences while being unique, but not over-the-top, in performance.

Indeed, the campaigns we've highlighted score big points in all of these areas. Sure they're cute, fun and different. But more important, each was built on several synergies by promoting multiple services – online shopping, wireless access, and free email – and embracing as wide an audience as it could.

# BRANDING TOGETHER

As a global Internet media communications, commerce and media company, Yahoo! cherishes its relationships with other brand-name companies and products, and works closely with many of them in a wide variety of co-branded campaigns in a variety of market venues.

During the summer of 2000, it teamed up with Pepsi for a joint online and off-line campaign titled PepsiStuff.com. The program included an under-the-cap promotion in which consumers collected points printed on some 1.5 billion self-serve bottles of Pepsi and its related brands bottles which they could immediately redeem online for prizes and online discounts from promotional partners.

Both companies, no doubt, have mutual admiration for each other's brands, not to mention the audiences attracted to them. As Dawn Hudson, Pepsi-Cola North American chief marketing officer, said in a statement: "We're out to connect with consumers in ways that really touch their lives. That requires being relevant and, in today's increasingly Web-connected world, few brands are more relevant than Yahoo!" (Yahoo! and Pepsi, joint press statement, March 22, 2000.) It also doesn't hurt that Yahoo! is popular among teens and young adults, a primary target for the soft-drink maker.

Yahoo!, on the other hand, saw a major opportunity to expand distribution into new channels with Pepsi, but focused its announcement on promoting its expertise in providing online and off-line marketing services through its Fusion Marketing services to such leading brands as Pepsi.

Other efforts to promote its marketing abilities and attract additional advertisers grabbed hold of other popular trends. In June 2000, Yahoo! reached out to the ad agency market by creating a "Whose Client Wants to be a Millionaire?" advertising contest. Contestants were required to develop the media and creative components of an integrated online marketing campaign using Yahoo!'s Fusion Marketing set of sales and marketing tools designed for media, communications, commerce and business/enterprise services. Each entry also had to include Yahoo! Broadcast as a media type.

A panel of judges – comprising such advertising luminaries as Ellen Oppenheim, senior vice-president and media director for Foote Cone Belding New York and Paul Kurnit, president and CEO of Griffin Bacal Inc – was formed to review the entries from ad agencies and in-house advertising departments. The winning entry, announced in early fall, received $1 million worth of advertising on the Yahoo! network. Jumping on the popularity of the "Who Wants to be a Millionaire" craze sparked by the success of the Regis Philbin-hosted game show isn't particularly cutting-edge when you think of it, but using it to attract the attention of ad agencies and in-house departments to showcase its Fusion Marketing services and hammer home the Internet as a powerful advertising tool certainly was an innovative twist.

Co-branded leveraging also has made its way into the sports and entertainment arenas as well. A major marketing relationship with News Corp. in 1999 connected Yahoo! with nine of the entertainment company's entertainment and news outlets. The launch targeted the 1999 Super Bowl Sunday with promotional spots and commercials during pre- and post-game programming. Yahoo! also sponsored the debut of Fox Television's irreverent and envelope-pushing animated series "Family Guy."

Other sports-focused campaigns included official sponsorship of the National Hockey League and the NHL Players Association that included an online ballot at Yahoo! Sports for the league's 49th NHL All-Star Game in 1999. One year earlier, the company's sports-related campaigns included daily news coverage and information on the Winter Olympic Games from Nagano, Japan, delivered in seven different languages.

Entertainment-related campaigns, often used to promote new types of media services, continue to embrace a diverse cast of characters and locations. Yahoo! has "been" to just about every awards show – Oscar, Emmy and Grammy – and major musical events from Webstock to Woodstock. Artists representing a wide range of musical styles – from the most recent teen sensations such as Jewel, Kid Rock, Flaming Lips and Squirrel Nut Zippers to more adult-oriented performers as Willie Nelson and The Blues Brothers – participated in the launch of Yahoo! Digital multimedia site through online concert broadcasts.

Entertainers and other celebrities have also played a major part in the company's continued support for numerous charities

designed to complement its mission to support greater awareness for community-based organizations around the world.
Charities such as the Elton John AIDS Foundation, the American Red Cross and the America Diabetes Association have all
benefited from celebrity online auctions or sponsorship of
other fundraising events.

## PRIVATE PARTS

Although Yahoo! wants you to know that it's indeed everywhere,
the company doesn't want to step on any virtual toes to get
that message across. It initially shunned such spam-producing
techniques as email reminders, push channels and other methods in its early days prior to the development of My Yahoo!
customization. And that strategy attracted its share of critics
who berated the company for not capturing valuable information about its users and, eventually, could not survive in the
coming age of one-to-one marketing.

As one critic noted in ZDNet UK in June of 1998: "Every
month, 25 million unknown users show up at this site … and
Yahoo! doesn't know who they are, where they live, what they
like – it's all anonymous. That strikes me as foolish." What's
interesting to note here is that the person making this statement is Seth Godin, founder of Yoyodyne, who would later sell
his company to Yahoo! and serve as its vice-president of direct
marketing for a time.

Nevertheless, Yahoo! has remained steadfast in championing
online privacy and continues those efforts as a founding
member of NetCoalition.com – a collective public policy group
comprising members from some of the leading Internet-based

businesses, including eBay, America Online and Amazon.com. In late 1999, the group launched its "Consumer Privacy Education Campaign" designed to generate greater awareness among online users regarding online privacy and directing them to resources and information to help them keep personal information off-line.

As Yang has noted, Yahoo! wants to empower users by helping them make informed choices regarding their privacy while online. "Our involvement in this campaign reflects our strong desire for all Internet users to have the pertinent information they need to make these educated decisions." (Company Press Release, November 9, 1999.)

## PERMISSION, PLEASE

Its devotion to online privacy education, however, is a shrewd bow to another key facet of its overall vision: permission marketing. As we noted earlier, Seth Godin may have chastised Yahoo! for apparent oversight of valuable marketing information a few years ago, but he later supported the company's vision through his own expertise in the emerging philosophy of one-to-one marketing.

Permission marketing, as Godin explains in his book of the same title (*Permission Marketing*, Simon & Schuster, 1999), is a hot topic for online marketing in the years ahead. Traditional marketing – what Godin calls "interruption marketing" – just doesn't do it anymore. Sure, companies like Proctor & Gamble created empires on such interruptive devices as TV commercials and telemarketer phone calls. He notes that P&G has worked it so well that it now "spends some $2 billion a year interrupting people."

# FIVE ELEMENTS FOR EFFECTIVE ONLINE PRIVACY

The Web is such a cool tool for data gathering and analysis. First you take the information obtained from online transactions and personal preferences, throw in some demographics, add a touch of "clickstream" data to map where users go online, and you now have a powerful individual buyer profile.

But smart marketers know that any misuse of that information – whether its real or perceived – can easily unplug customers while earning the wrath of government regulators and privacy watchdog groups. That's why more companies now devote much effort and energy to develop privacy programs, and even appoint someone to oversee online privacy.

Michael Kraus of Diamond Technology Partners, an e-commerce development consulting firm, believes the best privacy efforts incorporate the following five elements:

◆ *Notice.* Develop privacy policies that are concise and easy to read. Post them prominently on your site. Customers must know that are collecting and using information before they give it to you.

◆ *Consent.* Customers must actively consent to sharing information, and use of "I accept" and "I decline" buttons put control in the hands of users. Keep in mind that FTC guidelines state that only individuals over the age of 13 can give consent; younger children must provide verifiable proof of consent from their parents.

◆ *Access.* Once you collect the data, make sure customers have complete and continual access to it.

◆ *Security.* Passwords and other security measures must protect

customer-information databases and transmission of information. Only authorized "eyes" should be able to enter these databases.
◆ *Enforcement.* You can't just talk the talk. Integrate privacy policies into all your business processes, and make sure all employees read them. When violations occur, treat them as you would any other breach of confidentiality.
(Source: *Marketing News*, February 28, 2000)

As Godin notes, classic "interruptive" techniques were moneymakers in their time. Companies could spend a buck to interrupt someone and end up making $2. But these techniques are losing their spark simply because there are just so many messages being communicated to people these days. Experts say we can encounter some 3000 marketing messages a day. Nothing more than clutter.

And that clutter means less impact in swaying customers. Smart marketers know Internet has given consumers more power in how they seek out and ultimately select products and services. So the ability to get close to people is to get their permission to sell to them.

According to Godin, interruption marketing represents an expansion of marketer power. But today, such strategies must reflect the shifting of power to the consumer. And permission is one way marketers can cut through the clutter with messages that are anticipated, personal and relevant to the consumer. When properly delivered, competitors often fade into the background.

As Godin sees it, one of the biggest problems with online marketing right now is that companies are treating the Internet like television, and its costing them billions of dollars in potential online revenue. It's also sullying the attitude of marketers regarding the power of the Internet as a marketing tool.

But keep in mind that the Internet is nothing like TV – at least at this point. According to Godin, only 50 million people are surfing the Web on a good day, which averages to about 25 people per Web site. That's like having eight million TV networks instead of ten.

Although he admits that permission marketing is expensive to conduct, he also believes that following these key steps can help you to achieve better results that can generate an impressive return on investment:

◆ Figure out the lifetime of your customer, and then invent and build a series of communications that will turn strangers into friends.

◆ Be sure to carefully measure the results of each campaign, then eliminate the bottom 60 percent and replace them with new ones.

◆ Keep in mind in that it's much more efficient to use computers, rather than people, to send and receive information.

## POINTERS ON PROMOTION

Yahoo! is just about everywhere. And if they aren't there now, you can bet money they'll be there sometime in the near future.

Yahoo!'s "everywhere" strategy accurately reflects both its overall business strategy as a global Internet media company and its keen marketing sense that follows the basic tenets of successful promotion:

◆ *Have a good story to tell.* Your message can only be effective when it offers something that people want to hear. From its early days as the story of two whiz kids from Silicon Valley to its current role as a business leader in Internet media and commerce, Yahoo! always provides a good story. People want to hear what they have to say. Heck, it's the reason why we wrote this book!

◆ *Seek expert support to get your message across.* Yahoo! knew it needed solid support for its marketing strategies. Right from the start, the company signed on with – and listened to – agencies that not only knew how to market well but also had successful experience in marketing for the new Internet economy. Even as the company expands globally, it continues to seek the right promotional support. That's why Yahoo! signed on with a local public relations firm when it launched Yahoo! Korea. And, according to Karen Edwards, it continues to consider other more global agencies to beef up its current PR resources.

◆ *Create promotions that generate the best buzz.* Yahoo! is known for its creative and edgy promotional events which often appear more like parties than business events. And that's what makes them so effective. Despite their fun and irreverent appearance, their promotions never lose sight of the underlying business objectives. Yahoo! selects the best venues and creates experiences that are unique but not over-the-top. And they are designed synergistically with multiple audiences and multiple outcomes in mind. Take the example we mentioned concerning the parachutist making the online purchase in mid-air. This stunt was daring, edgy and reeked of the company's irreverent personality. But it also supported several business objectives, most notably Yahoo! Everywhere, while also appealing to growing audiences of online shoppers and users of wireless communication devices.

◆ *Leverage the power of co-branding.* You work so hard to create your brand, so why not use it in conjunction with other well-established brands to gain greater distribution and audience awareness? Not just any other brand will do. As Yahoo! shows us, you need to develop co-branding promotions only with companies that can help you establish greater credibility, increased distribution and exposure, or entry into an untapped audience or market.

◆ *Be respectful of your customers.* Yahoo! may be everywhere, but it's never "in the face" of its customers. Online privacy and permission-based marketing rule its promotional strategies, and for good reason. Those companies that overstep the boundaries and inundate an audience with unwanted messages will never achieve the interest or the respect of the audience they're trying to attract.

# REFERENCES

Anon. (2000) "Analyst Day Supports Yahoo's Plans to be Everywhere," NewsTraders Inc., May 19, 2000.

*Marketing Briefs, Marketing Educator*, American Marketing Association, Vol. 17, No. 13, June 22, 1998.

Frankel, Alex (1997) "How to Go Public When You Go Public," *Fast Company*, June 1997, Issue 9, p. 38.

Krauss, Michael (1998) "Launch Events Build Good Buzz for Startups," *Marketing News*, American Marketing Association, May 22, 2000 Vol. 34, No 11.

"Yahoo! Joins with NetCoalition," Yahoo! press release, November 9, 1999.

Godin, Seth (1999) *Permission Marketing*, Simon & Schuster, New York.

Krauss, Michael (2000) "Getting a Handle on the Privacy Wild Card," *Marketing News*, February 28, 2000, Vol 34, No 5.

Red Herring Staff, (1998) "Case Study: Yahoo! The Evolution of an Internet Startup," *Red Herring*, January 1998.

Nine

# CREATE A DYNAMIC CORPORATE CULTURE

B usiness *is* change. Technology constantly improves and transforms. New products and services regularly debut in the marketplace. Customers' needs and wants continually evolve. And the boundaries for doing business keep broadening through global expansion and strategic partnerships.

As much as we, as a society, talk about change, the reality is this: nobody really likes it. Change – we're talking the real, earth-shattering kind that looms threateningly on the horizon and keeps us up at night – often generates resistance among those most affected by it. It's only natural. Many of us have been raised to accept the status quo and work with it, not change it.

So it's no wonder that many companies are organized to resist major changes. But the reality is, businesses no longer have a choice. They can't just sit back and allow the startups – those with nothing to lose and everything to gain – to create all the innovations. Companies that don't change ultimately disappear.

Given this fact, it's even more important than ever for companies to create cultures that embrace the realities of change so they can respond more effectively when needed. Easier said than done, particularly for businesses entrenched in a particular way of doing things.

That's why Yahoo! offers such a valuable example for creating the type of company culture needed to remain competitive in today's – and no doubt tomorrow's – business environment. Although its roots were planted firmly in the free-spirit entrepreneurial soil of Silicon Valley, the culture has been nurtured through a unique combination of professional backgrounds and business experiences.

Given all of the accomplishments we've talked about in this book, you can't help but believe that Yahoo!'s corporate culture played a big role in making them happen. In this chapter, we'll look at the insights of several of the company's leaders and how they work together to build a truly dynamic working environment.

## ADULT SUPERVISION NURTURES DISTRIBUTED INTELLIGENCE

Although extremely knowledgeable about the Internet and its related technologies, Yahoo!'s co-founders knew little about building a business. In classic Silicon Valley jargon, they had the vision but they also needed "adult supervision" to take the company to greater heights.

Through a headhunter, they found such talent in Tim Koogle, who at the time was CEO of Seattle-based Intermec. Koogle was not your typical high-tech type, but his current responsibilities and previous experience at Motorola appeared to be a good fit. Koogle understood the vision and became a key player in its evolution.

Koogle supported the decentralized structure and the importance of distributed intelligence. He continually cites it as one of the reasons behind Yahoo!'s success. "It's not hierarchical,"

# DRESS DOESN'T MAKE SUCCESS

As we noted, Yahoo! rose from non-traditional roots. The high-tech businesses that sprang from Silicon Valley often produced cultures that focused more on people's ideas and their ability to make them a reality, rather than on how they were dressed for success in the workplace. A lack of traditional business attire became a hallmark of high-tech corporate culture that eventually made its way into the "casual" dress policies of other office environments throughout the country.

Yahoo! was a jeans, T-shirt and no shoes kind of place when it first started. In fact, co-founder Jerry Yang said he didn't even own a suit during the company's early days. Yang finally relented, however, when he had to go to New York for discussions on taking the company public. "It was dreadful," Yang said of his suit-shopping experience during an interview with the *Dallas Morning News* (June 18, 1996).

Co-founder David Filo echoed his partner's sentiment regarding business suits, opting not to even think about owning one. His reasoning: there's no reason why you should spend so much money on something you don't want to wear. A telling statement, coming from someone who had recently amassed a multi-million dollar fortune following Yahoo!'s IPO.

Yahoo! was also born from a mind-set that shuns traditional corporate structures and management layers. There are no hierarchies. Decentralization rules through an emphasis on distributed intelligence that applies the creative powers generated by small teams to meet performance goals. Team members usually work when they want, decide how they will work, and often work where they want.

And Yahoo!'s co-founders were more than happy to reflect these values with irreverent titles that reflected the company's culture. Yang's business card touts him as "Chief Yahoo!," and Filo later changed his designation to "Cheap Yahoo!"

The spirit of Yahoo!'s founders – emphasizing abilities over attire in a decentralized team-based work environment – laid the groundwork for the company's culture. But an influx of additional management insights soon came into play, prompted by the need to build a top-notch leadership team that could support its IPO, as well as maintain the vision of becoming a leading Internet media company.

he told The Motley Fool Radio Show in April 2000. "We do have a structure in the company because you need a structure to have some order on things, but it's a pretty flat organization."

The leadership team – which includes Yang, Koogle, and president Jeff Mallet – work in cubicles right next to each other. The layout has a purpose, as Koogle explained to author Charles Sigismund in his book *Champions of Silicon Valley*: "During a normal day, you'll find us hollering back and forth across the wall, bouncing around inside the cubes, grabbing each other and going off into a little conference room."

It's a tight operating team, according to Koogle, working much like three brains connected at the same time. And it's necessary since these three individuals make the decisions that run the business. "Between the three of us, we've made decisions on all deals that we've done that affected the company, be it strategic, raising capital, etc."

A typical leadership meeting finds these individuals, feet up on the conference-room table, talking about where they feel the company needs to extend itself and the possible risks involved. They seek opinions from each other. Although they may not reach conclusions at every meeting, Koogle sees these sessions as "seed planting" exercises that ultimately grow into future strategic directions.

But while the leadership team grapples with what the company is going to do, the actual decisions on how these strategies happen are driven out into the organization. Koogle believes this is a key component of Yahoo!'s culture, one that sets it apart from past generations of business hierarchies where most decisions have to flow up through the chain of command and then flow all the way back down the chain.

More important, driving out decision making fuels a dynamic environment that provides the speed and execution Yahoo! needs to support expansion and remain competitive. "Here we actually do distribute the decisions out to everyone who has authority to build great product and service," he told The Motley Fool. "What it means is you're making a lot of decisions in parallel, and what that means is you can execute faster. That's a real key in our environment because it's growing real fast, changing all the time, and there is a lot of competition."

# DARWIN WAS RIGHT: WHAT DOESN'T KILL YOU MAKES YOU STRONGER

The idea of driving decisions out within an organization rattles the very fabric of command-and-control management mentalities. Their reasoning: lack of control makes the company more open to failures. But that's exactly what dynamic business cultures thrive on – the ability to accept failures as a natural part of business.

When asked what were some of the most important lessons he had learned during his years in business, Koogle recalled a conversation with one of his entrepreneurial mentors when he was just starting out in the business world. He asked his friend what he believed was the secret behind his business success. The answer was astonishingly short and succinct: "Darwin was right." (*Champions of Silicon Valley*, p. 132.)

An interesting response, indeed. And it reflects a philosophy that everything – including companies – is part of an ecosystem. As Charles Darwin noted in his studies on evolution, things that are supported will grow, and those that aren't will eventually disappear. Change is an inherent part of the natural selection process, and each new organism represents an experiment. If the mutation can exist within the system, then it replicates itself and builds on those changes.

**Failure, in fact, becomes as much a part of the business process as success.**

Koogle believes the same model applies for businesses. "I'm a Darwinist. I believe in natural selection. Human nature is one of experimenting all the time, with innovation in technology, in social structure or whatever. The things that are supported grow, and the things that aren't fall away. So I think about business that way." (*Champions of Silicon Valley*, p. 132.)

Embracing such a philosophy in business requires an ability to consider failures in a totally different light. Failure, in fact, becomes as much a part of the business process as success. But can companies truly accept a culture that says "it's good to fail?"

Yahoo! does because it believes failures are the best way to learn tough lessons. The operative word here is *learn*. A failure can only prove itself valuable when people understand the reasons behind it and then apply this newly found knowledge for future innovations. That's why Yahoo! experiments with its Web sites. Many times changes arise from internal hunches or well-informed gut feelings about what could allow the company to grow within the Internet ecosystem, if you will. But very close attention is paid to the results.

Yahoo! is not alone in this acceptance of failure as part of the business growth process. Consider FedEx as another example. While most companies refuse to talk about failures within their businesses, FedEx is proud to discuss its ZapMail experience. During the mid-1980s, the company ran with an idea to create a same-day fax delivery service. Pricey fax machines were installed at key offices. But the effort proved disastrous, and reportedly cost FedEx as much as $300 million.

Now consider how this type of failure could impact future brainstorming sessions. It's safe to say that in many corporate conference rooms any new "radical" business idea would be greeted with a mention of ZapMail followed by the obligatory rolling of eyes. End of idea. Not so at FedEx. They see ZapMail as an example of the company's willingness to take risks and embrace change. Lessons have been learned.

Seth Godin, who served for a time as Yahoo!'s vice-president for direct marketing, following the sale of his company Yoyodyne, is another big champion of cultures that embrace change as part of the natural process. From his perspective, risk aversion seems inherent within large companies, but it seems to stem from cultural roots, not from the leadership. Commenting in a column in *Fast Company* (October 1999), Godin said he rarely hears complaints from big-company CEOs about employees who take too many risks or how they are spending more time on new initiatives than on core business. "And they don't complain about when people stand up and fight for ideas, standards and quality that they believe in," he wrote. "But they almost always talk about people who play it too safe, who avoid risks, and who ultimately are dooming their company to mediocrity and, ultimately, death."

## VISION LARGE AND SMALL

Risk aversion, however, often stems from a lack of vision that focuses beyond just what the business will do tomorrow. According to Koogle, "You need a vision that's large enough and grand enough so that there's something more than just tomorrow that people are working for. Something that inspires people." (Sigismund, *Champions of Silicon Valley*, p. 133.)

A dynamic workplace thrives on a vision that refuses to place a lid on what can be achieved. Workers should not feel shackled. A long-range vision, as Koogle sees it, generates feelings of freedom and inspires both himself and the people who work at Yahoo! But a vision that grows larger over time and possesses greater uncertainty can work against a company unless those within it have gained the confidence they need to make it happen. Everyone possesses different levels of confidence based on how they were raised, previous jobs they've had, personal chemistry and even what happened to them yesterday. A culture that allows people to take risks – to do something no one else has done before and achieve something from it – allows them to gain both experience and competence that increases their confidence level for even greater challenges.

That's why a vision must also incorporate a short-range component, which Koogle has said he focuses on a lot as a practical business approach. Any business, no matter which stage of development it's at, needs to proceed in steps. That way, you can more carefully manage how time is used. Naturally, companies want to invest time in areas that will achieve the highest rate of return immediately. But the trick is to strike a balance between what's creating returns today with what needs to be done for the future. "So you achieve a few things now, to build people's competence, and then you extend the vision. Then people feel confident and competent enough to extend," according to Koogle (Sigismund, *Champions of Silicon Valley*, p. 134).

> A dynamic workplace thrives on a vision that refuses to place a lid on what can be achieved.

## DAILY VISION

A connection between vision and daily work also allows you to more effectively manage available knowledge and resources throughout the various stages of business growth. It becomes much like a road map for achieving the larger vision. Every extension must be preceded by questions concerning the current structure and whether or not it can support a move to the next step. This helps to ensure that you are able to find and place the right people with the competence and confidence needed to make each extension work. Companies that fail to do this often suffer from disconnection that sooner or later kills the vision, as well as the company.

The best example of how Yahoo! applied this long- and short-range vision technique comes from its original business strategy. As Koogle noted, Yahoo! knew from the start that it could become a global Internet media company. That was the long-range vision from which it has never strayed. But the short-range vision provided the right steps – the daily experiments – to make it happen, as witnessed by incremental growth in community properties that built on the successes first achieved from its San Francisco site, as well as its methodical integration of various services and products into its network.

## Values drive the vision

"I saw people who ran very large enterprises who stuck to their values and wove vision and value together."
– Tim Koogle

So often we hear and read about business and values as conflicting elements. But Koogle has stated that the two are not mutually exclusive, and companies indeed have been built on philosophies that the two can work together. He's cited his experience at Motorola as an example. "From watching, I learned a lot of business principles," he said. "I saw people who ran very large enterprises who stuck to their values and wove vision and value together." (Sigismund, *Champions of Silicon Valley*, p. 137.)

Values initially come from a company's founders and top executives who are determined to do the right thing and believe that vision must be part of the leadership. From there, vision and values become woven into the company's culture, allowing other negative forces, such as greed and ambition, to dissolve into the background. Once instilled in the culture, peer pressure becomes a driving force in maintaining the values and the vision.

Say, for instance, your values focus on serving customers. As this value becomes part of the cultural fabric, people within the environment will only look outward, not inward. They will not seek solutions for the sole benefit of the company. Rather, they will look only for ways to provide better service, quality and value to customers.

But keep in mind that the key is to provide feedback so that people understand that what they're doing truly serves a purpose. Supporting the values will solidify the vision. This way, even when things change at your company over time, the principles and values behind the business remain constant.

Consider, on the other hand, how a lack of vision and values can play in the other extreme for companies who find themselves faced with do-or-die change situations. Godin has referred to this as "corporate grouchiness." (*Fast Company*, July 2000.) It generally rears its head as one of two common forms.

The first is complete denial. The company refuses to acknowledge that changes are actually happening in the industry. The feeling is that changes are nothing more than periodic bubbles in an otherwise calm sea. But when those bubbles begin to burst, startups and competitors quickly move into place.

The second offers an uglier scenario. The company knows that times are changing, but what the heck! It becomes open season on the cookie jar for top executives who grab profits while the profit taking is good. After all, they can still make their numbers look good because they are not investing in the future.

As Godin noted: "Hey, if your ship is going down, it might as well go down in style!"

## HOW TO KEEP YOUR CULTURE AFLOAT

As we've noted in this chapter, change is an ongoing part of doing business. Yahoo! has made change a part of its culture and applied it effectively in its evolution from a Web directory to a global Internet media company.

But we've come up with a few things you should consider in terms of building a new company culture that can respond to inevitable change, or how you can begin to transform your existing culture.

◆ *Focus on opportunities.* All discussions involving business change should initially focus on the potential opportunities for the company, not on how much it will cost, what the competition is doing, or what could happen to the stock price. Make change a positive driver within your culture – one that emphasizes possibilities, not liabilities.

◆ *Don't fear failure; learn from it.* Mistakes do happen. Things don't always turn out the way we originally planned. It's part of life, both personally and professionally. When mistakes do happen, forget the finger wagging. Use mistakes as an educational tool. Determine what went wrong and why it happened. The insights your company can gain will only make it wiser as you move to new initiatives and business ventures. Remember also that people who are not threatened by failure only get stronger from it.

◆ *Distribute decision making within your culture.* Although Yahoo!'s leadership team works closely on strategic vision, the ability to make the vision a reality is pushed down through the company. As Koogle has noted, you have to let the people who understand your markets and know what your competitors are doing be responsible for putting new directions and strategies into action. After all, those who are closest to the action have the knowledge and skills needed to make the best decisions on implementation and ongoing management. When companies fail to distribute decision making, executives and managers spend too much of their valuable time on execution, crisis management and consensus building. Rather, they should spend their time on thinking where the business should be going within the next year, two years or even five years.

◆ *Focus on the long term.* People also need to be able to focus on long-term goals (at least six months or more) and not just on making small short-term profits from the status quo. Denying a long-term vision puts your company at risk since it probably won't be able to see market changes or emerging competitors until it's too late. Give people the chance to look beyond what's going on tomorrow and reward those who create successes out of long-term strategies.

◆ *Don't forget the daily vision.* Let's be realistic. You can't ignore the day-to-day aspect of your business. After all, what is happening today determines whether or not you'll be successful in the future. An eye on the daily "experiments," as Koogle calls it, allows you to gauge the effectiveness of your current structure and whether it can support a move to the next level. It also allows you to more effectively monitor current resources that can be more quickly realigned to meet new ventures or challenges.

# REFERENCES

Cassidy, Mike (1996) "Out of Uniform," *Dallas Morning News*, June 18, 1996, p. 1ff.

Sigismund, Charles (2000) *Champions of Silicon Valley* John Wiley & Sons, New York, p. 129.

Godin, Seth (1999) "Guillotine or Rack?" *Fast Company*, October 1999, Issue 28, p. 341.

Godin, Seth (2000) "Change Agent," *Fast Company*, July 2000, Issue 36, p. 290.

Gardner, David and Gardner, Tom (2000) Fool Interview with Tim Koogle, chairman and CEO of Yahoo!, The Motley Fool Radio Show, April 18, 2000.

Ten

# STAY PARANOID

I n the words of Candice Carpenter – founder, co-chair and CEO of iVillage.com – Steve Case, Tim Koogle and Jeff Bezos are the most powerful people in the Internet industry today because they have proved the Internet business model. We would add that Case and Koogle have definitely scored bull's-eyes. However, the jury is still out on Bezos.

## DYNAMO TODAY;
## DINOSAUR TOMORROW

Staying on top in the high-technology field is uniquely challenging because of the pace of development, the speed of change and the don't-look-over-your-shoulder-or-you'll-see-who's-gaining-on-you mentality that's characteristic in the field. In fact, staying ahead in the Internet space is a little like laying down railroad tracks in front of a locomotive. You have to keep on looking ahead, work as fast as you possibly can and never look back or you might get flattened. Dan R. Bannister – chairman of DynCorp, a multibillion-dollar, employee-owned, high-tech company – preaches constantly that competition is different. "Today because of technology we compete with start-up companies. In the past they wouldn't have had a chance. The startups come up with creative ideas to compete (name your own price for airline tickets). Consider what MCI (now WorldCom) has done (to AT&T). Look what Microsoft did – giving away products free. That was a change that enabled it to leapfrog over its competitors. Who ever heard of giving your product away free? (Okay, let's say it. Yahoo! did. But advertisers paid them.) It caught the whole industry off guard. What do you do with a competitor what gives products away for free? It challenged everyone. I preach constantly that everyone is a change manager. I emphasize that positive change doesn't mean reacting to external forces, it means creating change. I tell people that at some place, some competitor has a bunch of people figuring out how to beat us. They're going to do something different and better than we do – changes that will make it a stronger competitor. Then we have to react to that.

**"I tell people that at some place, some competitor has a bunch of people figuring out how to beat us."**

**– Dan R. Bannister**

When you start reacting to changes imposed on you, you're usually trying to catch up. If you catch up, you're only even. Good competitors will constantly change the dynamics, culture, or circumstances of a market so they can be in control. We try to be proactive, initiating change that will cause our competitors to react. In almost every instance where we offer a proposal to a customer, we try to be innovative, to offer something different from what a competitor may offer."(Author interview.)

## "WE'RE ALWAYS PARANOID"

That's what Jerry Yang told a reporter for the *Christian Science Monitor* back in 1998. That feeling continues and probably for good reason, as we'll explain a little later.

It is tough to separate the paranoia from the culture of this company. It's been there from the start. And probably helped it grow so fast in the shadow of the mighty visionaries who surrounded it in Silicon Valley.

In fact, it seems to be a part of the culture of Silicon Valley. Just ask yourself what Bill Gates, John Chambers, Steve Case, Andrew Grove and the Filo/Yang/Koogle gang at Yahoo! all have in common. Paranoia. Lurking fears about things that affect their business.

Paranoia. It's the coin of the Silicon realm. And for good reason. The pace of change is so rapid that even Moore's Law – the tech commandment that says the power of computing will double every 18 months – has been subsumed under newer, faster principles, like the capacity and declining cost of storage. Storage capacity is doubling every 12 months and the cost is sinking like a stone in the Marianna Trench.

> "Business success contains the seeds of its own destruction. The more successful you are, the more people want a chunk of your business and then another chunk and then another until there is nothing left."
> – Andrew Grove

You have to stay on top of rapid change, monitor the competition continually and get so forward looking that you aren't caught just reacting to competitor initiatives. Do that and you're history.

Andrew Grove, corporate leader of chip titan Intel, one of the world's most admired companies, is generally credited with the saying "only the paranoid survive," and is author of a best-selling book by the same title (Random House, 1999). "When it comes to business, I believe in the value of paranoia. Business success contains the seeds of its own destruction. The more successful you are, the more people want a chunk of your business and then another chunk and then another until there is nothing left. I believe that the prime responsibility of a manager is to guard constantly against other people's attacks and to inculcate this guardian attitude in the people under his or her management." Grove worries about "products getting screwed up, hiring the right people, morale slacking off" and, of course, "competitors." Competitors can displace you with customers by building a better mousetrap or by doing things better, faster and cheaper.

## USE FEAR POSITIVELY

Fernando Espuelas, co-founder, chairman and CEO of Star-Media Network in New York, uses the fear of competitors positively. In creating the business he states: "the most important factor was our single-minded pursuit of success. We wanted to develop the Internet industry in Latin America. From the very beginning, our theory was that every 30 days we would have a major competitor in the marketplace. So, if we didn't create more barriers to enter the market every 30 days, we would lose. That didn't happen. But it was healthy for us as a company to have that kind of focus, that kind of drive – and that kind of paranoia." (*Fast Company*, January–February, 2000.)

Andrew Grove worries about what he calls SIPs or strategic inflection points that are like tectonic or discontinuous changes affecting the business. Sometimes they are technical in nature, sometimes not. The best way to deal with SIPs is to respond quickly. Even better is to cause SIPs to happen in your industry.

Aside from the founders' (Yang and Filo) natural instincts for survival, Tim Koogle brought a lot of the big business savvy to the table early on. In 1995, they sold a combined 15 percent interest to Reuters, Ziff Davis and Softbank, Koogle shared these thoughts about the transaction: "I brought a lot of the paranoia because I've been on all sides of the table. And I know how some of these big companies think. I also know that you ought to temper your paranoia because a lot of big companies have a great deal of baggage. There are things that they say they might want to do that they never can (and things that might prevent them from going into a new area such as culture, revenue reduction, cannibalizing existing businesses, and so forth). I've lived in there (having spent years at Motorola), and I've watched those guys, and I know that you can temper your paranoia – a little bit because there's ... excess baggage" which is a good thing. (Sigismund, *Champions of Silicon Valley*, p. 124–5.)

By overcoming its natural fear of these companies, Yahoo! was able to establish lasting and profitable relationships that resulted in them being able to rapidly expand content, open new markets with very little invested capital, add value for users, and quickly leverage their position in the Internet space.

A little aside for you readers: if you've read through to this point, you know this isn't a muckraking book. No reason it should be, because Yahoo!'s founders, who are all still with the company, have pretty much done everything right. The company is acknowledged as a core holding in any Internet-related portfolio. But we can tell you first hand they are still real careful about talking to people – for example, us. We tried several direct and indirect contacts at the company and no one would acknowledge either our emails or voice mails. At first we thought this was a little strange as we've done interviews for many publications and Web sites. Most of the time corporate officers or marketing communications people are extremely cooperative and often eager to speak with journalists and authors. So it was a little disconcerting that no one at Yahoo! would even respond to our emails or phone calls.

Authors can get a little paranoid, too. One of us – we won't say who – started to think: sure they won't respond because we didn't approach them at Internet World 2000, or we aren't with the *New York Times* or CNBC. Maybe it's because our publisher isn't big enough, or we won't be on Larry King Live. But that's no excuse. We still deserve at least a "no" and a reason. Fact is, without an introduction from someone they know, you probably can't get anybody important to return your calls in the Valley. They're just too busy. We'll just try not to take it personally. (Yeah, right.)

Sure the stock has been beaten down. But not like most of the other companies in its industry. Yahoo! is one of the industry darlings. And a street favorite as it continues to beat estimates and to increase advertising revenues – something that has been a problem for many other portals and dot coms. That's why it's down less than 50 percent. Some of its second-tier competitors are down 90 percent. Some have consolidated (like Lycos merging with Terra Networks). Some have gone back to their search engine roots (like AltaVista).

Understanding the guarded nature of the company on certain strategic matters, it's also fair to point out that because of the egalitarian nature of the Internet, there is already a lot of Yahoo! out there for easy access. Just going to the Yahoo.com site opens up quite a door to the company, for users, investors and even researchers. For example, if you are thinking of investing in the company you can, with a few clicks of the mouse go from the main site to Company Info, which takes you to Investor Relations where you'll find annual reports back to 1996. There are also current SEC filings required of all publicly held companies, and investor FAQs responding to such pointed questions as why the company purchased Geocities and Broadcast.com – and even the rationale for the acquisition of eGroups. To quote Michael Klein, president and chief executive officer of eGroups, "Group email is one of the fastest-growing Internet categories and is likely to touch the lives of virtually anyone with an email address. This acquisition by Yahoo! supports our mission to deliver the world's largest, easiest and most comprehensive group communications platform."

There are also links to additional SEC filings, press releases and individual email address for contacts within the company who will respond to those seeking further information (we don't guarantee that).

# LIVING IN A HOUSE OF GLASS

Another observation: The nature of the Internet with its tracking mechanisms, site maps, and real time feedback allows Yahoo! to see into its house as if it were made of glass. Everything is transparent to the user. The site is in full view as a web of links, threads and connections all over the world. And it's changing, evolving and mutating at a rapid pace. What's more, there are lots of other eyes out there studying the same diorama. Just one more reason to fear lurking competitors because the company strategy is pretty much transparent to the practiced unblinking eye.

# MINDING WHAT'S SAID PUBLICLY

Koogle has been quoted as saying in conversations that the company has always talked in measured responses when speaking to the press, shareholders and analysts about where Yahoo! is headed. They wouldn't want to sound too high and mighty or appear as being too cocksure of themselves. What's more, they don't want to be in the spotlight and certainly don't want to tip their hand to the competition. However, in *Champions of Silicon Valley* he admits to always wanting to "grow ... into a very large media business."

On July 13, 2000, Ziff Davis' Interactive Investor announced – almost in a footnote to its March 2000 perennially impressive quarterly gains – that Gary Valenzuela would retire from the chief financial officer's slot and be replaced by Susan Decker, the former global head of research at Donaldson, Lufkin & Jenrette. ZD's reporter noted that perhaps Valenzuela retired because he was "exhausted from continually downplaying Yahoo!'s potential and had commented in the prior quarter that its extraordinary growth rates were "unsustainable." (ZD Interactive Investor, July 13, 2000.)

# HARNESSING THE POSITIVE VALUE
# OF FEAR

So how do you manage fear?

First, identify it. If you can't identify it, create it. And use it to create positive results. Example: Andy Grove is good at creating or using fear to motivate people, according to Avram Miller, vice-president of business development at Intel, speaking at a round-table discussion at a *Fast Company* conference in Telluride, Colorado. Why?

"If you're honest with yourself, you absolutely should be afraid. The crucial difference is between institutional fear and individual fear. In our company, we don't want people to be afraid on the individual level. It's important for people to know that we're all there together. But on an institutional level, we're scared to death. We run our company with fear. Fear is one of the greatest motivators. In fact, Andy Grove is really good at creating fear when we get complacent. We'll create our own enemies if we have to – but the world is a fearful place as it is, so there are plenty of real reasons to be afraid."

> **"In our company, we don't want people to be afraid on the individual level. It's important for people to know that we're all there together. But on an institutional level, we're scared to death."**
> **– Avram Miller**

Another fear Yahoo! has identified, monitored, and managed well – one that has caused other leaders to rail behind closed doors – is hoof-in-mouth disease. Having somebody misspeak to Wall Street or worse yet, give away strategy to the competition. One *faux pas* can ignite panic selling on Wall Street or tip off a predator competitor prematurely.

So Yahoo! hired Karen Andersen whose many years of journalism and media experience equip her to handle the press, to deliver the tough-love speech to corporate managers, or reign in executives when needed.

# THINK THE UNTHINKABLE

While businesses are scrambling to keep up with high-speed change, there are certain behaviors that get them into trouble. According to Bill Costello, president of Thinkorporated and author of the book *Birdbrain: Using Creativity to Get What you Want* (Thinkorporated, 1999): "successful businesses tend to continue implementing the ideas that made them successful. But in a rapidly changing world, ideas often become obsolete overnight. What's worked in the past won't necessarily work in the future." To keep up, you have to "continually generate new ideas just to keep your head above water." That applies equally to General Motors, and to Bill Gates who is arguably the most successful businessman on the planet – at the moment. Although Gates is the richest and most successful businessman "he did not anticipate the Internet. Now he's scrambling to catch up." Microsoft.net launched in 2000. If Bill Gates can miss an inflection point, so can you.

Gates is now constantly worried about the future of Microsoft. And he's retired from the day-to-day business to concentrate on strategy. In a recent interview in *U.S. News & World Report*, he said: "Will we be replaced tomorrow? No. In a very short time frame, Microsoft is an incredibly strong company. But when you look to the two-to-three-year time frame, I don't think anyone can say with a straight face that any technology company has a guaranteed position. Not Intel, not Microsoft, not Compaq, not Dell, take any of your favorites. And that's totally honest." (*The Futurist*, May 1, 1999.)

# HOW TO REACT TO THE COMPETITION

Okay, so your competition is real and you fear they are making inroads. You're worried about employees jumping ship. What can you do about it? Here are some suggestions:

## A - You're small. They're big. What weapons can you use against big competitors?

◆ *Play up the headroom.* The freedom to be responsible and make decisions without having to submit them to a committee. Independence and empowerment have great psychic appeal to the e-generation.

◆ *Be flexible.* Break the 9 to 5 straightjacket. If Betty is a night owl let her hours start at 11 a.m. and end at 7 p.m. If Joe wakes with the roosters, give him a 7 a.m. to 3 p.m. shift. When people set their own hours they tend to work better and longer and be happier throughout the day. Be flexible about the offbeat, like bringing pets to the office. Case in point: a recent survey of over 6000 employees by the Roper Starch Research organization, noted that "while a competitive salary is an important consideration in today's tight labor market, the mantra of today's workforce is flexibility, flexibility, flexibility. Employers must recognize that employees want to balance competing responsibilities themselves." Further, it "found that 51 percent of employees would stay in their current job rather than switch if their employer offered flexible working hours. Also, 62 percent prefer a boss who understands when they need to leave work for personal reasons to one who could help them grow professionally. Perhaps most surprisingly, 51 percent of employees prefer a job that offers flexible hours over one that offered an opportunity for advancement (Roper Starch Worldwide, 2000). One shrewd high-tech company recently hired people to take care of personal errands its staff complained they didn't have time for, like runs to the dry cleaner, the laundromat and post office.

◆ *Emphasize the speed of decision making.* In large companies where consensus meetings or a participatory management style proliferate, decisions can take weeks and months and sometimes it seems their only purpose is to overthink things. Scott McNealy, CEO of Sun Microsystems, put it this way: "One of the biggest weaknesses of executives is that too many overthink things. The best decision is the right decision. The next best is the wrong decision. The worst decision is no decision." (*Entrepreneur*, August 2000, p. 87.)

◆ *Think about the environment you create for people.* Of course, with the shortage of talent and the surge in high-tech employment growth, there's always going to be movement. And your company is bound to lose someone to the competition. So keep a vigilant eye out for ways to keep the best employees happy. It's more than the money, the stock options and the incentives. But these won't hold people if that's all you've got. Especially if the company stock takes a hit like some of the dot coms experienced in the summer of 2000. (Big companies, take note. This may be a good time to rethink differences and ask the talented employee with underwater stock options back.) Managers must always think about how to improve the overall working environment, and how to inspire their workforce.

Twenty-five years ago, a fellow franchise operator of an employment agency was having great success while I was just scraping by. We were in similar territories. I went in to visit him and talk about what was working for him. Ted was an accountant. So I figured he was just better at the financials and accounting than I was. Turns out he had hired the best people to market and sell the agency and its services. And he did things like run out and get them coffee and lunch. He said to me: "Tony, I do anything I can for these good people because they are the ones who are building my business. I'll do anything I can to help make their job easier. If I run out and on the way pick up coffee and cake to keep them happy while sitting at their desks, that's good use of my time. I'm here to make sure they get everything they want. (PS – Ted went on to become the biggest franchisee in the New York metro area while I closed my branch a year later.) Today they call that "servant leadership" and it has been used to get sterling results from otherwise ordinary people. The classic servant leader was Jesus Christ, according to two new books released on the subject, *Leading by the Book* by Ken Blanchard, Bill Hybels and Phil Hodges (William Morrow & Co., 1999) and *Jesus in the Midst of Success* by Charles W. Morris and Janet E. Morris (Broadman & Holman Publishers, 2000).

◆ *Play up total involvement.* Many people – young bloods in particular – want more say and involvement in their destinies and are not content to just leave the rest of the product or service delivery stream to others. So if your key talent is a crack design engineer, emphasize how they'll play a part in the other areas like marketing and advertising. They may in fact know a lot about what the customer would find useful in the product and that may be helpful in promoting it to the user.

## B – They're small. You're a large, well-established, brand-name company. What weapons can you use against startups and small companies?

The best large companies have learned how to mimic small companies. They create smaller, more autonomous units. They offer greater wealth-creation opportunities for their best people, regardless of age or seniority. And they compensate these people on the basis of performance. The best companies also find ways to keep twenty- and thirty-somethings connected to the larger organization and to give them exposure to people at the top – all of which makes them feel that they are part of a smaller organization.

Big businesses can capitalize on their size. For instance, they've got more money, so they can afford to give a 35-year-old more responsibility and a bigger budget than small companies can. Big companies also have many more jobs to fill. More jobs means more bosses. So big companies can offer more mentoring opportunities (*Fast Company*, August 1998, p. 104).

# WHY THE UPSTARTS HAVE THE EDGE

It can't be overstated that the big company is at a disadvantage in the Internet world. Startups are emerging into the atmosphere every day. The only hope a large company has of attracting and keeping talent and not being undermined by a competitor is to think and act like a small company. It may be too late for some outfits but for those who have their antennae and directionals here's a competitive look at the big company/small company landscape and a list of the tactical advantages small companies hold, from Seth Godin, columnist for *Fast Company* and founder of Yoyodyne (acquired by Yahoo! October 1998):

◆ *Inventory*. This was traditionally a big company advantage. It dissolved when products moved online. Now you have a complete inventory of products available all the time – for example books and CDs. So the concept of the superstore that was a killer in its category has been neutralized.

◆ *Capital*. Access to funding for businesses used to be a who-you-know and who-knows-you kind of club, with the cost of entry the size of a telephone number. The threshold of entry has gone way down as the Internet has developed. Meanwhile, the amount of speculative capital that's available has risen to unprecedented levels while the amount of capital necessary to fund an online business has gone down.

◆ *Brand equity*. Used to be a major advantage, before the Internet. "Not anymore. For some reason that I don't pretend to understand, Web consumers resist existing brands." For instance, "Time Warner threw every magazine that it owned onto the Web, and yet Pathfinder still didn't attract a whole lot of consumers. Yahoo! News outdraws CNN.com every single day, despite CNN's relentless promotion of its site – all day, every day – on the number-one TV news network."

◆ *Customer relationships*. Industry leaders have been able to count on regular customers just the same way the local stores counted on consumers who shopped in the neighborhood to keep on coming back. Sad fact is the consumer has changed and can no longer be taken for granted. They will jump ship readily for "cheaper, faster, friendlier service online." It's as true for consumer or business-to-business relationships.

◆ *Employees*. Workers can do much better at a small company, for two reasons: the first is stock options. Large companies can't afford to make the same kind of offers that a small company can make. So big companies are doing things like spinning off assets and creating tracking stocks to boost value. As a result, the cost of keeping people at large companies is skyrocketing. (Editorial note: and the response will probably be to try and recapture rising costs by cost cutting, a surefire, short-term band-aid, and long-term failure.) The second is the Free Agent Nation and the technology that allows more and more experienced people to work from home with a low-cost computer, an Internet connection, a speedy print and copy center nearby and voicemail. Big companies no longer have a hold on the most talented people. Many are willing to do their best work and simply move on when the project is over.

# SURVIVAL TIP:
# ACT LIKE A SMALL COMPANY

If all this puts you past the point of paranoia and into fibrillation, take heart from Godin's final words:

"Even if you do work for a big company, it may not be too late to start acting like a small company. You may still have time to realize that the assets that you count on are disappearing – and to work hard to put yourself out of business. And if you work for a big company that won't listen to you, then it's time to leave. Hurry! Put your former employer out of business – before someone else does!"

# A LOOK AT THE FUTURE
# OF THE INTERNET

If the Internet has taught us anything, it's that the future is unpredictable.

Competition grows fiercer as the Internet grows and evolves into a true mass-market medium. Jerry Yang says "the Internet forces you to be always changing." Business plans quickly become obsolete in such a fast-paced business environment. You must think big and move fast. At the time of this writing, the emergence of wireless Internet access and hand-held Internet devices is forcing Internet companies like Yahoo! to rethink its services and develop new outlets to support it.

Seth Godin was once asked to schedule an interview with a large company in several months to talk about where the Internet would be in three years. While the big companies are busy forming committees, gathering and studying the data and analyzing it in order to make some decisions, you can be experimenting, trying new things, dropping what flops and developing new businesses.

Before looking at the future it's worth noting some recent facts about how radically traditional business has changed. In the early 20th century, the autos and the oil companies started to dominate the industrial scene. By 1993, GE passed Exxon as the world's most valuable company. Consumer goods passed industrial products. In 1998, Microsoft overtook GE in market valuation. So the PC supplanted consumer goods. In 2000, Cisco became the world's most valuable company. So the Internet supplanted the PC. In the 20th century, a trend that

# WHY BIG COMPANIES SHOULD BE PARANOID – AND ENTREPRENEURS SHOULD BE BOLD

◆ *Fear of failure.* At big companies, risk aversion is institutionalized. "When the big boys at ABC, CBS, or NBC make a big mistake, everybody notices. Here's what you big-company types need to understand: The folks who are gunning for your company are on a suicide mission, and they couldn't care less about whom they might bring down with them."

◆ *Small fry customers are a big catch.* "Customers who aren't worth Cisco Systems' time, or AT&T's, or McKinsey & Co.'s, are fair game for you. By focusing on small businesses and small opportunities – which happen to be growing fast – you can thrive amid the much bigger competition."

◆ *You're the president of the company.* You'll pay much more attention to your customers and you'll value them much more than a big company can.

◆ *R&D "Rapido."* The Internet is moving too fast for all of the meetings and studies that big companies insist on. You will think and move fast while they are still figuring out things like who'll take minutes of the meetings.

◆ *Customers like underdogs.* "Customers know that you're going to try a little harder, work a little longer, and value them a little more. You'll have a better attitude, and nobody will choose to do business with big, arrogant companies when there's an alternative."

◆ *Low overhead.* Big companies simply can't match little or virtually no overhead models.

◆ *Decision making.* What really needs to be said here? Big companies lose people everyday over this one "tar pit" alone. And here is where small firms, with their lean internal processes, shine.

> ◆ *Time.* As a small company you have to time to work on the impor-
> tant things since you won't get pulled away by impromptu meetings
> and committees designed to suboptimize the decision-making
> process, and you can get things done much more quickly.

dominated for about 70 years was succeeded by a new trend
that dominated for seven years and was displaced by a new
trend in two years.

## What's next?

Well, even the experts do a lot of hedging here. Understand-
ably so.

However, one thing is certain: tomorrow will be different. And
tomorrows come faster than yesterdays. Overall trends that
seem to be important now are handheld devices that offer
the convenience of connection to the Internet, anytime and
anywhere. Another trend is convergence and the rise of a super
network of networks delivering information and knowledge
power to anyone and everyone at anytime and in anyplace.

How will this happen? Partly through the creation of smart
wireless handhelds with embedded intelligence and a universal
software platform that enables any handheld device or appliance, no matter what brand or function, to hook together
seamlessly into a single network. Partly through things that
haven't even been thought of yet. Whatever develops and
wherever the trends and technology take us, Yahoo! seems
certain to have a hand in.

# THE FUTURE OF YAHOO!

Most recently the company has got a big push on in the B2B marketplace. Yahoo! launched its B2B marketplace in the summer of 2000, announcing its plans on the very same day as America Online – typical of the kind of neck and neck nanosecond leads you have on the competition in the industry.

Is anything out of the realm of possibility for Yahoo!? From an investor point of view, probably not much. Yahoo! has evolved from a hierarchical directory of Web sites to a search engine to an Internet media company offering new, entertainment, electronic mail and shopping services to electronic commerce, and now, business to business. They will keep on plugging away no matter what tomorrow brings. As Jeffrey Mallet, president and COO recently said in an interview with the *Dallas Morning News* about future initiatives on the heels of it's integration of Broadcast.com: "Someone referred to us as like termites. You don't see us, and then all of a sudden we're into a marketplace."

> "Someone referred to us as like termites. You don't see us, and then all of a sudden we're into a marketplace."
> – Jeffrey Mallet

Right now Yahoo!'s future is as bright as ever. The Motley Fool, a top Internet investor Web site, listed five key reasons why they consider it one of their portfolio favorites.

◆ *Explosive growth.* Yahoo! remains in hypergrowth mode with revenue and earnings growth of over 100 percent year over year. Customer growth as measured by daily average page views, unique visitors and registered users are all growing at over 100 percent year over year. Email, voice, media and wireless growth are just starting to enter the momentum phase. Of the Fortune 50, 29 are advertising clients.

◆ *Dominant leadership position.* The company continues to expand its position as the Web's most dominant portal. And its growth is dominant internationally as well as domestically.

◆ *Strong cash flow.* With its low capital expenditures and exceptional level of cash flow growth it's likely margins will continue at high levels.

◆ *Flawless execution of its business model.* As they say in the technology field, execution is key to success. Execute well or be executed. And Yahoo! continues to execute on a shrewdly simple model of being "the enabler of connectivity and transactions." It avoids any acquisitions or initiatives that require high capital spending so its "amazingly lean business model stays intact."

◆ *Expanding possibilities.* "The ever-growing value of the Yahoo! brand, and the close relationship the company builds with its customers may give Yahoo! the highest option value of any company in the world today." It's got great possibilities for global expansion. Already into its 23rd global property with the launch of Yahoo! India where Internet users are projected at 11 million by 2003. Yahoo! Japan is on the momentum track. And 40 percent of Yahoo!'s traffic now comes from international sources. It continues to expand its mobile network and device partnerships with recent additions like AT&T Wireless, Taiwan Cellular, Siemens, Telecom Italia Mobile, Virgin Mobile to name a few. Plus new capabilities in Yahoo! Messenger, Chat and Clubs. Plus new services such as Yahoo! Player, a streaming media provider of digital music and video files. Plus new initiatives in the business enterprise area, Corporate MyYahoo! A customized enterprise information portal based on the My Yahoo! interface that will be marketed to corporate customers for an annual fee. Plus the eGroups acquisition, adding 17 million international users and 8000 message groups. Plus joint ventures in consumer commerce with Kmart (bluelight.com) and a co-branded free Internet service featuring content and services for Spiegel. And the icing on the cake may be:

◆ *Focus*. The single-minded pursuit of its sharply focused goals. (Excerpts from Motley Fool Research, a report on Yahoo! by Zeke Ashton, available at www.Fool.com/research, July 26, 2000). As Jerry Yang says: you always have other options. So the purple and gold army will probably never get too cocky. Andy Grove would be proud.

Do you Yahoo! yet?

If not, you probably will.

# REFERENCES

Grove, Andrew L. (1999) "Only the Paranoid Survive," Random House, 1999.

Sigismund, Charles (2000) *Champions of Silicon Valley* John Wiley & Sons, New York, pp. 124–5.

"Make Money by Thinking the Unthinkable," *The Futurist*, May 1, 1999.

*Employees Speak out about Soft Benefits, Results of a Study of 6000 North American Workers*, Roper Starch Worldwide, 2000.

Scott Smith interview with Scott McNealy in *Entrepreneur*, August 2000, p.87.

Fishman, Charles (1998) "The War For Talent," *Fast Company*, August 1998, p. 104.

# AFTERWORD

## The story continues ...

The saga of Yahoo! by no means ends at this point. The Internet, after all, has only just begun to make its impact in the global marketplace. Leading companies will continue to evolve along with the technology; others may fall by the wayside – it has already begun – as new competitors come into play.

As authors, we tried to keep our hands on the pulse of Yahoo! for as long as we could, given our publication deadline. But knowing the dynamic nature of this company we have profiled – not to mention the Internet business world in general – it's a sure bet that new initiatives and strategies have emerged since our manuscript went to press – even with the fast cycle time of our publisher.

We are, however, still keeping an eye on the company and its progress. That's why we invite you Yahoo! watchers to visit our Web sites to catch up on the latest news and insights regarding the company. We've also set up an online discussion board for you to add feedback, questions and comments about this book, as well as your personal insights regarding the company and the guiding principles that have made Yahoo! a leading Internet portal and commerce site.

For more information, visit Delphi Publishing at www.delphipublish.com/yahoo or McFadden Communications at www.mcfaddenweb.com/yahoo.

Here's to your business success!

Many thanks,

Anthony Vlamis (tvlamis@delphipublish.com)

Bob Smith (bsmith@mcfaddenweb.com)

# INDEX

## Other titles in this series: